Conversations with Graham Swift

Literary Conversations Series
Monika Gehlawat
General Editor

Conversations with
Graham Swift

Edited by Donald P. Kaczvinsky

University Press of Mississippi / Jackson

The University Press of Mississippi is the scholarly publishing agency of the Mississippi Institutions of Higher Learning: Alcorn State University, Delta State University, Jackson State University, Mississippi State University, Mississippi University for Women, Mississippi Valley State University, University of Mississippi, and University of Southern Mississippi.

www.upress.state.ms.us

The University Press of Mississippi is a member of the Association of University Presses.

First printing 2020
∞

Library of Congress Cataloging-in-Publication Data

Names: Swift, Graham, 1949- interviewee. | Kaczvinsky, Donald P., 1960-
    editor.
Title: Conversations with Graham Swift / edited by Donald P. Kaczvinsky.
Other titles: Literary conversations series.
Description: Jackson: University Press of Mississippi, 2020. | Series:
    Literary conversations series | Includes index.
Identifiers: LCCN 2020001545 (print) | LCCN 2020001546 (ebook) | ISBN
    9781496828453 (hardback) | ISBN 9781496828460 (paperback) | ISBN
    9781496828477 (epub) | ISBN 9781496828484 (epub) | ISBN 9781496828491
    (pdf) | ISBN 9781496828507 (pdf)
Subjects: LCSH: Swift, Graham, 1949—Interviews. | Authors, English—20th
    century—Interviews. | BISAC: BIOGRAPHY & AUTOBIOGRAPHY / Literary
    Figures | LCGFT: Interviews.
Classification: LCC PR6069.W47 Z46 2020 (print) | LCC PR6069.W47 (ebook)
    | DDC 823/.914 [B]—dc23
LC record available at https://lccn.loc.gov/2020001545
LC ebook record available at https://lccn.loc.gov/2020001546

British Library Cataloging-in-Publication Data available

List of Books by Graham Swift

Novels by Graham Swift

The Sweet-Shop Owner (1980)
Shuttlecock (1981)
Waterland (1983)
Out of this World (1988)
Ever After (1991)
Last Orders (1996)
The Light of Day (2003)
Tomorrow (2007)
Wish You Were Here (2011)
Mothering Sunday: A Romance (2016)

Short Story Collections

Learning to Swim (1982)
England and Other Stories (2014)

Nonfiction

Making an Elephant: Writing from Within (2009)

Contents

Introduction

In *Mothering Sunday: A Romance,* Jane Fairchild, a novelist in her nineties who has lived through every decade of the twentieth century and risen from housemaid to bestselling author, considers the same tiring and repetitive question asked by interviewers over the years, "So when—so how did you become a writer?" Jane toys with the interviewer, giving a surprising but unimpeachable answer: "At birth. At birth, of course." The interviewer senses a certain "slyness" in Jane's face, and Jane's gaze suggests a counter-question: "You think I would tell you a lie?" Jane then ponders if, since she is a storyteller, anyone ever wonders whether her responses are simply another story. Yet the answer, she knows, satisfies and since it has been told many times before, she cannot change it now. Rather than lying outright, however, Jane is selective in her responses, and there is one story that she will never tell: the story of her "Mothering Sunday" in 1924, when, left alone in the library of her lover's country house, she realizes her calling as a writer.

And who can blame her? After all, she would have to divulge sensitive personal information and private feelings in a public forum, opening her up to unnecessary and unwanted scrutiny and criticism. Some matters are best left unsaid. The scene aptly illustrates some of the complex psychological interplay that must necessarily take place during any author interview; and though Graham Swift adamantly denies any autobiographical elements to his stories, something of the same thoughts and concerns must have passed through his mind during the numerous interviews over his more than thirty-year career. He provides a somewhat more credible, if just as evasive, answer to a similar question posed by Lewis Burke Frumkes. "Well, I think," states Swift, "the evolution would have started pretty early on. I was around twelve, thirteen, when I first began to want to be a writer, which is a different thing from discovering that you have any talent to be a writer." In fact, Graham Swift has never been comfortable with interviews and feels that an author should ideally be "invisible" in his writing. Swift tells Robert Birnbaum, for instance, that his sense of a writer in his early career "was essentially of this person you never saw. They might have a photo on the back of the jacket of the book, but they sat somewhere and they wrote and they delivered their books to a publisher who published their book and meanwhile the writer remained where they were and possibly carried on with another book." But he admits that this situation has changed dramatically in the contemporary world of book publishing, and, for him this has "taken some adjusting." Although he does not enjoy the format, however, this collection of eighteen interviews attests to the fact that he often accepts the obligation, if reluctantly.

Swift has suggested that the best interview is the one that forgets it is an interview and becomes a conversation. Generally, he takes interviews in a local—his favorite is the County Arms, "a big barn of a pub," near his home—or a London restaurant, rather than in a radio station or before a large audience. And for the most part, the conversations are pleasant and the interviews proceed with great predictability. Those who have interviewed Swift consistently find him courteous, quiet, deliberate, and self-effacing in manner. One notable exception in this collection is the interview with Eileen Battersby for *The Irish Times*. Here, Swift is decidedly (and uncharacteristically) irritated with the interviewer over her unflattering review of Swift's novel *Tomorrow*, especially her dislike of the narrator Paula Hook. While Battersby remembers her previous interviews with Swift as "enjoyable," she writes that this one seemed more of a "college tutorial." Another source of tension is the topic of influence, particularly after Swift was accused of plagiarizing William Faulkner's *As I Lay Dying* without acknowledgment in his 1996 Booker-Prize winning novel *Last Orders*. From this collection, however, we can see that as early as 1985, Swift admired Faulkner's novels, especially *As I Lay Dying*, as well as the works of George Eliot, Charles Dickens, D. H. Lawrence, Ernest Hemingway, and Thomas Hardy. As Swift tells Catherine Bernard in a 1995 interview, just prior to the controversy over *Last Orders*, "I find the whole business of having to declare your influences more and more troublesome." The bad publicity made Swift more cautious and, at times, defensive in his answers to interviewers during the late nineties.

In some of the interviews, Swift is caught off guard by an unexpected question or comment. A relaxed conversation with Patrick McGrath, Swift's friend and fellow writer, suddenly becomes awkward when McGrath blurts out: "Do you think it's all right for middle-aged men to run off with small female antelopes?" The question refers to the character of Uncle Walter in Swift's short story "Hoffmeier's Antelope." Swift can only reply: "Well, they don't." But he recovers quickly. "It was all right for him [Uncle Walter]. I might be wrong in saying they don't." At other times the interviewer shows a remarkable lack of familiarity with Swift's work. This is particularly true in early interviews or when Swift is interviewed by Americans. In the second interview of this collection, for instance, Don Swaim interviews Swift in New York City while on a promotional tour for the American publication of *Waterland*, which had been short-listed for the Booker Prize. After suggesting that Swift's style is similar to Raymond Carver's and urging Swift to read Carver's short story collection, Swaim confesses that he finds Swift's writing somehow "unEnglish." Swift is clearly flustered. After a moment's hesitation, he recovers and states "you'll have to explain that." The irony is pointed, and the humor (which Swaim apparently misses) characteristically Swiftian, for *Waterland* primarily concerns the very difficulty of "explaining" anything. Tom Crick, history teacher and narrator of the story, must "explain" why Freddie Parr, his boyhood friend, ended up drowned in a lock. The novel even has a chapter entitled "The Explanation of Explanations." Swaim's own "explanation" of his observation is less than convincing and a bit condescending. He suggests Swift's writing does not compare to any English writer in terms of its "economy" of style. Swift, with great literary acumen, suggests his writing may be close to that of the contemporary short story writer Ian McEwan. Finally, Swaim, after backtracking, states that he has recently been reading Richard Adams and Dick Francis, only to admit that he does not "have that much of an expertise about British writers." And yet this interview is also one of the more revealing about Swift's early career and influences, his relationship with the group of celebrated writers who emerged in Britain during the early '80s, the sources of both his novel *Waterland* and his second novel *Shuttlecock*, and Swift's approach to writing as an act of the imagination. But as the interviewers become more familiar with Swift's work and Swift learns to anticipate or deflect the questions asked with greater confidence, the interviews become more relaxed and philosophical, more of a pleasant talk over a beer than a professional grilling.

Indeed, against Swaim's assertion, Swift now seems one of the most English of writers. Born on 4 May 1949 on the borders of Sydenham and Catford, South London, Graham Swift was brought up in South Croydon and attended Dulwich College as a scholarship student. Even though his novels often involve a tension between parents and children, Swift characterizes his childhood as happy and untroubled. In 1967, after taking a five-month hiking journey on the "hippie trail" across Europe, through Greece, across the Aegean, as far as eastern Turkey and back, Swift attended Queen's College, Cambridge, where he studied English literature, graduating in 1970. For his post-graduate degree, Swift went to the University of York, working ostensibly on a thesis about the role of the city in nineteenth-century English literature, though actually spending much of his time writing stories. In 1974, he taught in Volos, Greece, while writing what he admits was an "irredeemably awful" novel. He returned to England the next year and worked at several jobs, earning his living primarily by teaching English and grammar at O and A levels in a "further education college." Only with the success of his third novel, *Waterland*, in 1983, was he finally able to give up teaching and earn a living writing full-time. He currently lives in Wandsworth with Candice Rodd, his long-time companion whom he met at York and married on 29 February 2000.

Graham Swift is the author of ten novels, two books of short stories, and one work of non-fiction, *Making an Elephant: Writing from Within*, a collection of autobiographical essays, interviews, and poems. His life, in one sense, has been remarkably uneventful; and Swift rarely provides personal details, perhaps because there is very little to tell. As he states consistently throughout these interviews, he awakens early and is generally at his desk by 6 a.m., writes with his fountain pen, and leaves off around noon. He will return to his desk after lunch, especially if things are going well. Although Swift travels on promotional tours, he prefers a sedentary life, sticking close to his home in South London. He admits, in an interview with Jamie Andrews, that he is not a "great traveler." However, he qualifies this statement by noting that he does travel a lot in his head, for "the traveling that a writer does is not necessarily from one country to another. It's from one character to another." His is a regular, unvarying regimen, the workaday schedule of a professional writer. After his first three novels, which were published in fast succession, from 1980 to 1983, Swift has published on a slow but steady basis, approximately one novel every four to five years. He has not written plays or for other media, though three of his novels have been made into films, and he occasionally writes poetry, though he confesses that he is not a poet. His one hobby is fly-fishing, and "Fishing in Literature" is the subject of his edited collection with David Profumo, *The Magic Wheel*. As he tells Ramona Koval and Jamie Andrews, it is also through his interest in fishing that Swift became good friends with Ted Hughes, whose own archive faces Swift's in the British Library.

On the surface, then, Graham Swift, in his manner and experiences, is quite ordinary. Yet this ordinariness masks a rich imagination and a penetrating intellect, which can craft some of the most engaging stories in the language. He is, in many ways, the "writer's writer," with an attention to narrative voice, formal complexity, and stylistic precision. One of the questions interviewers often ask Swift is whether he bases his novels on his own life and if the characters are fictionalized accounts of himself or people he knows. In an interview with a group of students from Düsseldorf University, focusing on *Last Orders*, Swift states: "No, I don't think I was inspired in that direct way by people in a pub, if only because I make up my characters. I certainly don't base my characters on people I know personally or on people that I meet or I see." He also does little pre-planning or preliminary research for his works, but relies upon instinct and his own imagination, though he will verify the credibility or accuracy of details in a plot or scene after the novel is drafted. Until there is a biography of Graham Swift we will not know how credible these statements are and, of course, he is a storyteller of the first magnitude. For now, Swift's unconventional advice to young writers is also one of his most memorable principles—write about what you don't know.

But if there is no direct correlation between Graham Swift and his characters, we can recognize that Swift writes about what he does know: the people who live in the city of London, particularly South London, and its suburbs. That said, some of the most memorable scenes in his novels take place outside the city, in the Fens of East Anglia or the countryside of Kent. Often the main characters are older than Swift himself, members of not his, but his father's generation, and the central event in their lives, whether directly or indirectly, is the experience of World War II, what Swift has called, in an essay on his own father that appeared in *Making an Elephant*, "the extraordinary period." Generally, these characters are white, middle- to upper-middle-class men: the kind of male characters who inhabit the suburbs of London where Swift grew up and lives. In a few instances, Swift considers the working classes, like Jack Dodds, master butcher of Smithfield, and his mates in *Last Orders*, or the upper classes, like the Nivens and Sheringhams of *Mothering Sunday*. He rarely includes minorities or immigrants, those communities that are changing the political, social, and cultural landscape of England in the late twentieth- and early twenty-first century. Swift has also been criticized for his lack of strong or memorable female characters, though Amy Dodds, Paula Hook of *Tomorrow* and, especially Jane Fairchild in *Mothering Sunday*, are notable exceptions. In fact, his attention to the female voice is one of the major developments in his later writing. He also avoids directly commenting on or depicting current or controversial political subjects, which he sees more as the realm of journalism, even rejecting the notion of a "contemporary" novel. He tells Stef Craps, for instance, "I don't think there is such a thing as contemporary fiction. The great strength of fiction is that it isn't and cannot be contemporary, because of the time it takes to write." While the settings of his novels may be circumscribed and the range of his characters somewhat narrow, his themes are universal: death, love, history, parent/child relationships, the power of the imagination, the role of storytelling, and the consequences of knowing. Ultimately, like William Wordsworth in *Lyrical Ballads*, Graham Swift's writing is meant to make the ordinary extraordinary.

This project began as an intertextual study of Graham Swift's novels that, in a Swiftian digression, quickly required me to dig deeper, to reclaim, as it were, the siltation of the author's own thoughts and ideas. Before I could move ahead, I had to go back, and, in doing my research, I became frustrated over the inaccessibility of primary materials. This collection of interviews is, then, the product of the arduous process of scholarly dredging and is meant to be a useful resource for critics as well as a source of genuine interest for his ever-growing popular readership. While I have tried to include at least some commentary on each of his novels, I have given greater attention to interviews on his best-known novels, *Waterland* and *Last Orders*. I have included interviews printed in English as well as some translated from French and Spanish. I have also tried to represent a wide range of formats, from lengthier interviews published in standard academic journals, to interviews for radio, newspapers, and, more recently, podcasts. Although Swift conducted his first interview in 1983, because of copyright restrictions, the interviews in this collection begin in 1985 with Swift's arrival in New York to promote *Waterland*. It concludes in 2016 with an interview by Jason Steger that appeared in *The Sydney Morning Herald*, where Swift contemplates an encounter with his fictional creation, Jane Fairchild, whom he admits is quite real to him, though, of course, he knows "this can't occur."

I would like to thank my editors at University Press of Mississippi, especially Katie Keene and Mary Heath, for their consistently good advice on how to proceed in the sometimes-tortuous landscape of copyright and permissions. Jamie Andrews, archivist at the British Library, was tremendously helpful whenever I emailed him. I am grateful to Louisiana Tech University for providing financial support for this project through the George E. Pankey Endowed Chair in English, which was made available through the State of Louisiana Board of Regents Support Funds. A special thanks goes to my wife Julia, who accompanied me on this journey (as on many others) and was always willing to listen.

Chronology

1949	Born Graham Colin Swift in South London on 4 May, second son of Allan and Sheila Swift of Sydenham; family later moves to South Croydon.
1960–66	Attends Dulwich College as scholarship student.
1967	Takes five-month journey through Europe on "the hippy trail," ending in eastern Turkey. On return journey buys Penguin translation of Isaac Babel's *Collected Stories*.
1967–70	Starting in October, attends Queen's College, Cambridge University, graduates with a first in English.
1970–73	Post-graduate education at University of York, writing short stories and discarded novel while working on his thesis on the city in nineteenth-Century English literature. Meets Candice Rodd, an undergraduate, his future wife.
1974	Teaches English in Volos, Greece.
1975	Returns to England and lives first with his parents and then with Candice Rodd. Supports himself in various jobs, including security guard, janitor, farmworker but primarily as part-time teacher of English.
1976	Publishes first short story in the *London Magazine* with encouragement from Alan Ross.
1980	*The Sweet-Shop Owner* is published.
1981	*Shuttlecock*, wins Geoffrey Faber Memorial Prize for fiction (1983).
1982	Publishes first short story collection, *Learning to Swim*.
1983	*Waterland* is published, which is short-listed for Booker Prize and wins *The Guardian* Fiction Prize, the Winifred Holtby Memorial Prize, and the Italian Premio Grinzane Cavour (1987) for Best Foreign Fiction; with success of Waterland begins writing full-time. Named, along with William Boyd, Ian McEwan, Julian Barnes, and Kazuo Ishiguro among others, in *Granta*'s "Twenty under 40," *Best of British Young Novelists*.

1985   Edits with David Profumo, *The Magic Wheel: An Anthology of Fishing Literature*.
1988   *Out of this World* is published.
1991   *Ever After* is published, which wins *French Prix du Meilleur Livre Étrange*.
1992   Film of "Waterland" released, directed by Stephen Gyllenhaal and starring Jeremy Irons, Sinéad Cusack, Ethan Hawke, and John Heard.
1996   *Last Orders*, winner of the Booker Prize and James Tait Black Memorial Prize for Fiction.
2000   29 February, marries Candice Rodd.
2001   Film of "Last Orders" released, directed by Fred Schepisi and starring Michael Caine, Thomas Courtenay, David Hemmings, Bob Hoskins, Helen Mirren, and Ray Winstone.
2003   *The Light of Day* is published.
2007   *Tomorrow* is published.
2009   *Making an Elephant: Writing from Within*, a collection of personal essays, poems, and interviews; British library purchases his archives.
2011   *Wish You Were Here* is published.
2014   Publishes second short story collection, *England and Other Stories*.
2016   *Mothering Sunday: A Romance*, winner of the Hawthornden Prize (2017).

Conversations with Graham Swift

Interview with Graham Swift

John Kenny Crane / 1985

From *Cimarron Review*, vol. 84 (1988): 7–12. Reprinted by permission of Beverley Crane.

This interview was conducted during Graham Swift's American promotional tour in the last week of April of 1985. His highly successful novel *Waterland* was due to be issued in paperback by Washington Square Press; and his three earlier works—*The Sweet-Shop Owner*, *Shuttlecock*, and *Learning to Swim*, a collection of eleven stories—were to appear for the first time in America.

Crane: Now that the time has come for you to make yourself publicly available in America, are you enjoying it or are you reluctant to be doing so?
Swift: Obviously, I enjoy it. This is my first visit not only to New York but to the States, and it's very exciting. I wish I had more time to see the sights. I enjoy meeting with people and talking—like now. There are certain things I find difficult and silly. Particularly the interview where the person who's interviewing hasn't read the work, which happens a lot, or the kind of interview in which you have two minutes to condense your entire oeuvre and views on it. I'm not terribly comfortable with a lot of publicity. It doesn't come naturally to me. I suppose I realize it is part of the job nowadays. A writer who wants to have a readership really can't afford to disdain entirely a little bit of what I'm doing now. It has been very exciting for me to get published abroad both here and in Europe, and translation is a very exciting thing to be subjected to.

Crane: Do you feel that your three novels and the stories in *Learning to Swim* all revolve around a common theme? I mean especially the tendency of our characters to judge reality as not worth living in and therefore to imagine another reality to actually exist in.

Swift: I think I'd accept that. Maybe I'd approach it in a different way. I almost always write in the first person, so my narrator is often as important as the narrative. That central character is usually somebody in a state of crisis, and thus the story he has to tell has about it a great deal of urgency if not necessity. It's as though the character has lost hold of experience, has suffered the shattering of some illusion perhaps, realizes he no longer can see his life in the orderly terms he might have done before. And he's in a position of having to put together the pieces, and he does so via the process of telling a story. And I do see storytelling as having that very crucial and therapeutic purpose.

Crane: You seem to thrive on finding these stories anywhere—a sweet shop owner, a clerk in a dead cases office, a fenland ragamuffin. Do you believe there is a story worth telling in every person and every place?
Swift: Yes, I believe that very strongly. There isn't a kind of area of life which can be turned into a story and other areas which cannot. There are stories everywhere, even in the most unlikely and unpromising situations. That's why I think I will always roam around in my beginnings of stories and in my characters, why I won't be heading back to the East Anglia of *Waterland*. I believe very strongly and very passionately in storytelling itself, in its value as a way of coming to terms with this world and what we experience, what we suffer, what we undergo. I think few things could ever replace it. That's why I have a great faith that the novel, which people are always saying is dying a death, that it never will expire, there will always be a place for it. I think it is the form where one can combine like nowhere else the world of ideas with the concrete world of things and sensual experiences. One can put everything into a novel. The ideal novel, the point at which a novelist can say that I can go no further, is that impossible point where you say everything.

Crane: Tell me, if you would, about the early stages of your writing career, the preliminaries of your recent successes.
Swift: I began to want to write when I was about fifteen or sixteen and began to do something seriously about it when I was twenty or twenty-one. My parents were very good in encouraging me despite the fact I was the first writer in the family. It took another ten years before my first book was published, so I had the long struggle, the rejection slips, the sending of things to magazines, the hoping and so on. The first story I had published would have been in 1976, I think, in *London Magazine*. I had sent

a number of stories to them which were sent back but with encouraging noises. Finally, they accepted one. The editor there was very good to me. At an early stage he wrote to me and said he thought I must be writing a novel. That was telepathy, because I was. He encouraged me with that. He said he would publish the novel, *The Sweet-Shop Owner*. Unfortunately, he ran out of funds, but promised to help me get it published elsewhere. After a long time, it found a home. It was at least three years between completion and publication. Which I don't think is such an uncommon story. Most of my short stories were written before *The Sweet-Shop Owner* and virtually all were published before *Shuttlecock*. They are early work, which worries me slightly because over here the stories are appearing after later work, and I don't think it would be generally understood that the stories are earlier.

Crane: Can you tell me what irresistible literary influences you are conscious of as you write—not that you are imitating but that you are conscious of speaking through you?
Swift: Well, if we were to talk of *Waterland*, the obvious other writer at work in that novel is Dickens. Thinking of the stories, I suppose a mixture of short story writers. I read, as most young writers do, D. H. Lawrence's short stories, which I think are greater work than his novels. I have been influenced by them and by Hemingway's short stories. Fairly standard things. There is a book of stories by a Russian writer by the name of Isaac Babel, and I read those in translation many years ago, and I remembered being very excited about them. Not for a moment did I attempt to imitate him; he was one of those writers who inspire you to write, and that is the most important kind of influence.

Crane: Is there no Faulkner in your work, as so many critics and reviewers have liked to suggest?
Swift: I found the response here that Faulkner is very present in *Waterland* interesting, because I certainly didn't think of Faulkner as I was writing the book. Now I have read some Faulkner, though not actually a lot. I do admire greatly *As I Lay Dying*—I think that is one of my favorite novels. I have read *The Sound and the Fury*, some of the stories, *Light in August*.

Crane: Not *Absalom, Absalom!* though?
Swift: No. Which is the one which has often been adduced as behind *Waterland*. The way I read this is that it is probably a natural American

response because Americans are more familiar with Faulkner, and they would see in the book Faulkner's writing. Faulkner is not much studied in England. Hemingway is the classic influence from America. And Fitzgerald.

Crane: I thought I felt the presence of Laurence Sterne in *Waterland*. The narrative voice seemed particularly Sternean.

Swift: Yes, I think that would be fair enough. The element of *Waterland* which, as it were, "plays around" with narrative, which says "oh let's stop this and have a digression here," does, I think, come from my liking not just for Sterne but of a lot of eighteenth-century baroque writing which enjoys that sort of digressive and diffuse approach. My own namesake, Jonathan Swift, does the same thing. And I like a lot of seventeenth-century prose which is sort of mock scholarly—rich in reference and encyclopedic.

Crane: Among contemporary writers, whom do you admire?

Swift: I could name one writer who lives in England, though he is in fact American by birth. A man called Russell Hoban, who I think is an extremely original talent. He's written some remarkable books, and his use of language and his ideas are quite extraordinary. Thinking on more international lines, I am in the good company of a number of writers who have been influenced by Márquez; *One Hundred Years of Solitude* is another book which just bowled me over when I first read it. It has meant a lot for me. Günter Grass is another writer whom I admire and think I'm influenced by. Amongst contemporary Americans possibly no one I'd like to single out. Bellow maybe. Heller possibly. But only in that rather oblique and "yes, I've read them" way. I think Heller's *Something Happened* is a very admirable book.

Crane: What about John Fowles? You are a very inventive writer, as he is at his best. Do you enjoy his work?

Swift: I don't think I would say I'm a wholehearted admirer of Fowles. What I admire about him is his wonderful narrative gift. He has a way of making you want to turn the pages; there's a tremendous pacing of his narrative. I've got some reservations about *The French Lieutenant's Woman*—the historical recreation in that is possibly a little too overdone and a little too self-conscious. And I am not very happy with the ending of that book.

Crane: William Golding?

Swift: William Golding I admire, though I haven't read everything by him. Books which stand out for me would be *The Inheritors* and *Rites of Passage*. Golding, too, has a wonderful narrative ability, a wonderful descriptive ability. In recent years, apart from winning the Nobel Prize, I think he's had a bit of a rough patch. His recent work doesn't seem to be up to his best level.

Crane: Would you agree with a feeling I have that we in America have more respect for the contemporary writer than the British have?
Swift: Yes, I think that's true. The writer in Britain is not a highly respected figure. We are not admired. Quite unlike France, where a writer or an artist in any field is generally speaking a highly respected figure, someone who has something important to contribute. Not so in England. The Irish, too, have a more natural artistic element in their character. The British are, for all their great traditions, literary and artistic, still a rather Philistine people, rather distrusting of the arts. It seems to be something we haven't managed to overcome.

Crane: Can you describe your creative day for me, the day in which things go well for you in your writing?
Swift: Normally, I'm a morning person. I can be starting work even before seven o'clock and I rather feel that if things haven't happened by, say, ten o'clock that that day may not be a productive one. There is that delightful oasis each day before the mail arrives and telephone can ring when things can happen. On an ideal day I would work right through to one or two o'clock, stop, have lunch, then, depending on how I felt about things, either call it a day or decide that this is one of those days when I must chew away at what I had done in the morning. I always have an abiding fear of stopping, of losing the thread; that sometimes makes me carry on when it would be better if I stopped. Friday is a slightly anxious day always, for I want to leave off at point when things will start happening again quite easily on Monday. I worry all weekend that I won't be able to.

Crane: What is a good day's productivity in quantity for you?
Swift: It wouldn't be very much, so I have come to accept. A page of writing, longhand, pen-and-ink writing, would be not more than five hundred words. I would be content with that.

Crane: Let's talk, if we could, about your present work. Do you have a compulsion to or a fear of imitating *Waterland*, its great success and its vast landscape and population?
Swift: Categorically no. I don't see that happening. I think I created a rich world in *Waterland*, but in what I write next I would like to create another somewhere else. There'll be no more Cricks and Atkinsons in future books.

Crane: What are you writing about at the moment, if you are willing to say?
Swift: I'll have to be fairly sketchy. I don't like to say too much about a book in progress, and also because my own sense of things is pretty sketchy, too. What I am doing is trying to get another novel off the ground with a sneaking suspicion, I suppose, that this may not be the novel that will eventually take to the air. I'm really at a stage of thinking and note-taking and general brooding and contemplation about something rather than getting chapters down, and I'm hanging fire a bit because I'm not sure this is the one. This is the first time in my writing career when there has be a pause, and I think a healthy one. When I finished *Waterland*, I was pretty tired. There has been a period of recharging the batteries. Combined with, I have to say, an element of feeling that *Waterland* was my breakthrough novel, my first successful novel in commercial terms. It's got me a reputation, and there is a pressure on what I do next. I have an act to follow, and instinct tells me I shouldn't follow it too quickly.

Crane: You have, however, continually demonstrated a propensity to write about childhood and parent-child relations. Do you think this will change?
Swift: I don't have children, but I am obviously very concerned with the fact that writers are people for whom childhood experience has not lost its meaning. The sensibility of children is still incorporated in an adult way of seeing things. Perhaps it is the sad fate of too many adults that their childhoods are lost.

Crane: Finally, let me ask you this about all your work. What are readers, reviewers, critics, all of us, missing in your work that you wish we wouldn't miss?
Swift: Good question. I think sometimes they're missing humor. I am often made out to be a writer with very bleak and pessimistic views, which there is some truth in; but I do hope there is, especially in *Waterland*, entertainment, fun and humor. That gets overlooked sometimes. Also, I love to see ambiguities. If I wanted to say that certain things are so, and absolutely so, I don't think I'd be a novelist. Novels are not about this or that but about this *and* that and about varieties of possibilities and contradictions and paradoxes, all these things which, as everybody knows, our real experience of life is. I am not a sociologist or a documentary merchant. I am a novelist. Which means I accept complications.

Don Swaim Interviews Graham Swift

Don Swaim / 1985

From *Don Swaim Collection, Box 4, Cassette 41*. Reprinted by permission of the Mahn Center for Archives & Special Collections, Ohio University Libraries.

Graham Swift, author of *The Light of Day*, *Waterland* and *Ever After*, journeys from London to visit New York for the first time. He considers himself fortunate that he is a full-time writer and does not need a second job. Once a teacher, his book sales rose enough so he no longer needed a second job. Swift discusses another job he once had working in a mental hospital. Don Swaim and Graham Swift also discuss what, if any, viable alternatives there are to mental hospitals.

Don Swaim: Two days in New York, have we been hard on you?
Graham Swift: I have been busy, but it has been pleasurable too.

DS: Tell us some of the things you've been doing.
GS: I have been talking to the media. I have been talking to *Newsweek*, various papers, radio. I've met a lot of people, been wined and dined, and seen a little bit of the sights of New York.

DS: Is Pocket Books taking good care of you?
GS: I think I could say they are, yes. [laughter] A sigh of relief. [laughter]

DS: This is your first time in New York?
GS: It is, it is. First time in New York. First time this side of the Atlantic.

DS: Has it been a culture shock?
GS: Well, it's a, a lot of it is familiar in a sense, because in England we pick up on a lot of American things. But nonetheless, it's a foreign country. I feel that, and here we are talking the same language, which is fun.

DS: Yes, and New York is not representative of the rest of the United States.
GS: I imagine that yeah.

DS: I come from the Midwest, and I came directly to New York from Baltimore where I worked for about four years. Before that, I went to school in the middle West. So I came to New York. One thing I noticed was that many of the people, most of them it seemed to me, didn't speak English. [laughter] And they look different; they sound, even the English-speaking people in New York, sounded different. Have you ever seen the Bugs Bunny cartoon?
GS: Yes, yes. I know the voice you mean, yes.

DS: Bugs Bunny has a Brooklyn accent. So I found the accents very harsh, very difficult. And I found people very abrupt. And it was . . . the currency seemed different somehow. The prices were all out of line. Sometimes I would go into a restaurant and look at the menu and look at the prices and say this can't be right. They were three times what I paid in France. So I am not sure that New York is representative of the United States.
GS: Yeah, I can see that is the case. You are talking about meeting people here and speaking English in New York, but that, for us, makes New York more European. I've already met people who I asked, "Are you from New York, here in New York?," and they say, "Yes, I'm from New York." And then they'd add afterwards, "Well, actually I'm from Poland, or I'm from Italy," and that whole background of people coming over from Europe possibly makes New York more like any European city, than anywhere else in the States.

DS: There's a poster shop, and you'll see them all over town, especially if you're in midtown, and you'll see a New Yorker poster. There's a cover of *New Yorker* magazine, and it shows an elongated Manhattan.
GS: Right.

DS: And then you see the Hudson River and then you see the rest of the country. It's as though the world were built around one little island, and you can walk across it in twenty minutes, thirty minutes. And yet New Yorkers have a warped perspective of the rest of the world. They don't see that there is a big nation beyond the Hudson.
GS: Uh huh.

DS: And they're not even sure there is very much across the Atlantic.
GS: Wow. [laughter]

DS: Did you grow up in London?
GS: Yes, I was born in London. Most of my life I've spent in London, except for student days. I was at Cambridge and then York. That's old York, not New York, and I spent a year or so abroad, in Greece. Otherwise, in London.

DS: They call York the White Rose City.
GS: Yeah. Lancaster is Red Rose.

DS: There is also a York, Pennsylvania and a Lancaster, Pennsylvania.
GS: Right. Oh, I think all the English towns are represented over here, somewhere or other. You've got a Manchester, Birmingham everywhere.

DS: You went to Cambridge. What did you study at Cambridge?
GS: I studied English at Cambridge. And I went on to York to do post-graduate research. So that accounts for getting on with six years of my life. And then I got right away from academic things. It was really only at that point, after university, that I got down seriously to writing. I don't regret my university life because I think I read more at that time than I have ever done since, and that reading is obviously something that has influenced my writing.

DS: Are you writing full time?
GS: I am now. When I started off, I was really in the position of teaching myself to write. I mean I don't think I had a natural flair for it. I think it had to be worked at. And given that and given that it is very difficult to be a young aspiring writer, I had to eat. I had to do something else. So I was a teacher on a kind of part-time basis. That's to say when I started out, I was teaching more hours than a full-time teacher and, as my writing got into print, as I got more confident with it, I reduced the number of hours until finally with thoughtful ends, I took a complete break, and gave up teaching. I hope that will last. I mean I don't think of myself as a teacher. I've no vocation as a teacher. I've always wanted to write, and I'm happy to say that I'm a full-time writer. Very few writers in England are in that fortunate position. But it is an insecure occupation, and who knows if I'll have to go crawling back to the classroom.

DS: What level were you teaching?

GS: Well, I was teaching what we call O and A level, I don't know if that means anything over here. The kind of college, well we call it a further education college, that means effectively that I was teaching young adults who had left school but who had not passed exams at school and were coming back for a sort of second chance. Mostly people in their late teens, early twenties. But, theoretically, and sometimes actually, people of sixty or more.

DS: English?

GS: Yeah, English.

DS: Grammar?

GS: Literature. Literature and Grammar.

DS: In the stories in *Learning to Swim*, they're most winning, and, as I was reading the stories, and, in fact, as I was reading the very first story in the book, "Learning to Swim," the title story of this volume, I was struck by how much you resembled the work of the American writer Raymond Carver. Do you know his work?

GS: I don't. I don't. I've heard good things of him though. But I haven't read a single piece by him.

DS: Well as soon as you leave here, you should head directly toward Doubleday or to Scribner's and pick up a copy of the short stories called *Cathedral*, his latest book.

GS: Right.

DS: There are tremendous similarities between your work and his. I was struck by these similarities. One of the chief similarities is the economy of your language. You do not waste words. In fact, your writing seems, I hate to say this, but it seems un-English.

GS: I mean, you'll have to explain that.

DS: I don't perceive of English writers writing in the style you have adopted. Now I perhaps am wrong because, obviously, I don't read every English writer there is. I just don't see English writers writing that way now. Maybe this is my own lapse.

GS: You are talking about the economy of language.

DS: The economy of language.
GS: Concision.

DS: The language that you are employing in your work.
GS: Yes.

DS: Are there parallels to your work in England?
GS: Well, obviously, I hope I'm my own man. I'm individual. But I think I'm a little surprised by what you say. I would imagine that because I am English, you know, spent most of my life in London, that my style would have an English flavor. I'm trying to think of some other writers of short stories for comparison. There is a short story writer called Ian McEwan. I don't know if he is heard over here. I imagine that he is published over here. He is a quite concise and economical writer. But the picture I am getting is that your impression of English writing is of something more elaborate.

DS: I suppose I probably should not have said that. [laughter] I don't know the relationship. I don't know that much, but I've been reading Richard Adams for example.
GS: Right.

DS: It is not too applicable to what you write.
GS: Right.

DS: Dick Francis is a mystery writer. Certainly does not write in the way you do in terms of content. But he is an economical writer. He is in a newspaper person. And in the jockey industry. So he does write in the economical sense. Bernice Rubens, I talked to her. Now she is . . . Well, let's go on, I really should, I bit off more than I can chew because I don't have that much of an expertise about British writers. But your work did strike me because it seems like a lot of the work that I am reading now in the United States, because a lot of people are patterning their material after the style of Raymond Carver. Who, by the way, has not written a novel. He writes short stories.
GS: Right, right.

DS: Have you written poetry?
GS: I have, a long time ago, and, uh, I think it is best forgotten. I dabbled in poetry at a relative early age. To tell you the truth, I don't know, but this is what I found out when I attempted to write poems, how poems are

written, that's to say certain very obvious technical things, like where do you stop one line and start another are really not within my ken. I'd like to think that . . . well, I think that prose can become poetry. So I'd like to write the kind of prose which could now and then flower into something like poetry rather than write poetry which descends into prose. But I've got no aspirations at the moment of writing poems.

DS: Mr. Swift, your first novel was *Waterland*, [*sic*] which has just been published in paperback in the United States. Tell me how this, you were teaching at the time, I imagine this is when you began working on this novel, tell me how this novel came about?

GS: Well, so far as I can keep tabs of this and remember, I'd say there were two stages. The first stage, as often happens at the beginning of things for me, is that some scene lodges itself in my mind and it won't go away and it seems to imply other things, it seems to have potential. Now how that exactly comes about is a total mystery, but in the case of *Waterland* I did have this image of a drowned body, and the body of a young boy—teenager—and I had an image of this happening in a remote situation, in a remote country, and some time ago. That is to say, I can't explain why that got ahold of me but it did. And that certainly wasn't what got the novel going, it was just something that I had on ice. And the breakthrough, the thing which made the novel happen was that I had the body and I had the various characters who discovered the body, including someone who I thought of as telling the story, who is the character Tom Crick in the novel, who is the same age as the boy who has died; and I wanted to come forward in time, the death occurs in wartime in the 1940s, and I wanted to come forward and think about what happened to my narrator figure later in life; and it was the point where I made him a history teacher that things took off, because then I had not only a man in later life looking back on what proved to be a crucial moment in his early years and something which influenced the rest of his life, but I had a man who was interested in the past in a wider sense. History. And I was then, so I realized, writing a novel about ideas as much as about drama, plot, and story. I mean, for me, the story is the most important thing. I mean I see myself as a storyteller primarily, but *Waterland* certainly has a great deal to say about the phenomenon of history. And if one is going to deal with such a subject you've got to deal with it from the point of view of some individual who would naturally be pretty obsessed by that subject. So it was a history teacher that really set the whole thing going.

DS: Graham Swift, in *Shuttlecock* and in a number of stories in *Learning to Swim*, there is a feeling, an undercurrent of madness.
GS: Yeah.

DS: Of insanity, the father in *Shuttlecock*, of course, is in a hospitable and does not speak. I'm not even sure about the narrator of the story.
GS: Right, he's a little unstable, let's say, right.

DS: In *Learning to Swim*, I had the feeling well, the narrator of "Hotel" was in a hospitable and in "The Tunnel" I had this feeling the young couple was in an abandoned building and were out in this, I guess, courtyard, and I had this feeling that something is wrong. What were they doing in this building? There were other examples as well. So I just wonder, why this apparent preoccupation with insanity that seems to be in your work?
GS: Well, it is certainly there. I could add to your list. There is an asylum in *Waterland*, which figures now and then. Well, I suppose my answer would be that there is a lot of madness in the world. I mean you only have to look up some of the things that happen in the world to see that the world is not an entirely rational place, and I shrink this down to the irrationality of insanity. Madness, at an extreme level perhaps, ought to be faced, ought to be explored. I think by exploring it we learn about ourselves and we learn to control the irrational element in our behavior.

DS: This is the same thesis that Gordan Lish uses, editor of Knopf, and a very skilled short story writer. He has published one short novel called *Dear Mr. Capote* and a collection of short stories, stories, not unlike your own. He had had a personal experience with insanity, and he usually writes from the viewpoint of one who has been insane.
GS: Yeah.

DS: Has insanity touched your life in any form?
GS: Well, happily, I don't think I have ever, in the clinical sense, gone crazy. I certainly have been irrational in my time but haven't we all. I did work once in a mental hospital. When I was a student I spent one summer working as a ward orderly in a hospital, and it was certainly one of the most educational experiences in my life. To go into this other world, which was pretty enclosed, and to see the other side of experience. These . . .

DS: These were one of education you say. I think it must have struck you emotionally.

GS: I think it must have done, yes, yes. And whilst it's true that I don't generally write in an autobiographical sense, I like to imagine and invent things. Certainly in *Shuttlecock* where there is a character, the father of the narrator, who has experienced this extraordinary breakdown, and no longer speaks and is indeed in a mental hospital. That hospital in the book is largely based on the one that I worked at, and the system, for example, patients who are admitted as though in a couple of weeks they were going to be okay and they were going to leave but they find themselves shifted along a series of wards which lead eventually, in some cases, to more or less permanent confinement, and that was something I saw and witnessed and was very disturbing. And I don't think society, though I can't speak for over here in the States, but I don't think in England we have yet evolved a happy way of dealing with insanity. A happy way of integrating it into ordinary, so called ordinary and normal society.

DS: Well, our mental health "experts," I put the term experts in quotation marks, feel they have solved the problems here because we have miracle drugs.

GS: Hm.

DS: And so we give miracle drugs to insane people and put them back out on the street. So you'll walk through the streets of New York City, and you'll see people talking to themselves and defecating in the street and performing all sorts of bizarre acts. It's not illegal. At least they won't arrest you just for being bizarre, talking to yourself.

GS: Right.

DS: You didn't see this a number of years ago because people who talked to non-existent beings were taken and put away.

GS: Yeah . . .

DS: You didn't see them. Now they allow you to see them. I don't know if this is the case in London.

GS: Well, certainly the use of drugs is pretty widespread as a treatment, and drugs don't always cure, they just eliminate the symptoms. The problem is, it seems to me, that once the drugs or whatever the treatment is, have done their immediate work, and somebody is sent out into the world again, there isn't sufficient after-care. And to go back to this place where I worked, there were a good many patients who were admitted for treatment, went out again, and because they couldn't finally make that adjustment back to the normal so-called world, they voluntarily came back to the hospital, they chose to come back because it was a place they felt safe in, which is a very sad state of affairs.

DS: When you were a child growing up in London itself, is that correct?
GS: Yes, in the suburbs of London, yeah.

DS: What were your interests? Was there some inkling in your young childhood that you might someday write?
GS: I, well I would say, that I, my ambition to write began when I was in my teens. But these things form maybe subconsciously at a very early age. I know that in primary school, so I'm told, because I can't remember this clearly, but I used to, my parents say that my teachers at primary school say I was particularly good at writing little stories even then. This is when I was about, I don't know, nine, ten, eleven years old. Certainly once the ambition crystalized I never had any doubts about it. It's what I've always wanted to do.

DS: Did you grow up in a bookish family?
GS: I didn't. No, no. In my immediate family, certainly, there is nobody else who is in the least bit literary. I was quite independent and original in that sense. I would say that my parents never stood in my way about this ambition to write. There are a lot of parents I think would, given that it's such an insecure course to pursue. But no, I can't find another artist figure in my family. And . . .

DS: What has been the reaction of your parents to your work?
GS: Well, they're certainly very happy now, now things seem to be working out very well. I think it's true to say that they've never entirely understood my writing, my preoccupations in my writing. But they've always been very sympathetic to my doing it.

DS: Do you know Martin Amis?
GS: Well, I don't know him. I've met him. I've talked to him very briefly now and then.

DS: I was talking to him last week. His father as you know is Kingsley Amis, and Kingsley just cannot stand Martin's work.
GS: That I know, yes, yes. [laughter]

DS: Martin was saying that Kingsley likes stories that start out "There was a shot in the dark." [laughter] Kingsley Amis thinks that Dick Francis is the greatest living writer in English today.

GS: Well, that I didn't know, that I didn't know. But I did know that there was this literary antagonism between the father and the son. I mean it must be, in one sense it is obviously a great advantage to be the writer's son of another famous writer, but I think it is more of a disadvantage, because one has to prove that one is one's own man.

DS: That's terrible when you think about it, trying to follow in the footsteps of a famous writer.

GS: Right.

DS: Famous American writer, Howard Fast, whose son Jonathan Fast is trying to make it as a novelist, and he seems to have adapted well to be overshadowed. Susan Cheever, a short story writer, father John Cheever is dead now.

GS: Right.

DS: She has written three novels and a memoir about her father. And they seem to be doing okay, going out writing completely different things. Jonathan Fast writing science fiction. Howard Fast known primarily for his historical and generational books. So, I guess as one tries to emulate the work of the parent who is going to follow that field, he would be in trouble, striking out as you mentioned on that. The Booker Prize is pretty soon, I think a year ago, I see that you had been nominated for a Booker Prize. That's a very valuable award to have in terms of book sales. Isn't it?

GS: It is. Yes. It's really the only institution of its kind that in England has some public impact on behalf of serious fiction, and over the last few years, the last four or five years, it's become extremely influential. And all the British publishers get very worked up around autumn, fall, when the prize is announced, and they are very keen to get books short-listed. To be even one of the nominated authors, let alone the recipient of the award, means a great deal in terms of public recognition and of sales in bookstores. It has its, um, side that perhaps one could criticize, I mean because it does select these six novels each year and give them a lot of attention. It means that a lot of other good books that are published at the time get overshadowed. And, but I think, in general, it has meant that now in England more people are reading good fiction than they did, let's say, ten years ago. And fiction is having a, generally, a kind of revival in Britain.

DS: I wonder about the awards, sometimes any award, whether it's the American Book Award here, the Pulitzer Prize, because they do, as you mention, miss books. Joseph Heller wrote the book called *Catch-22*, which is even a phrase in the English language.
GS: That's right.

DS: And the book came out in the early 1960s, it received a few reviews, but it was received poorly. Nobody bought the book to speak of, it languished for a couple of years, but gradually people began to buy it. It didn't quite go out of print, especially people on college campuses they began to buy it, and it is now a classic. But isn't that strange that here is a book that came out and nobody liked it. It was black, a piece of black humor, nobody liked it, and it took some thinking to see where that book stood in relation to other books of its time. Sometimes a movie will come out, a motion picture will come out, and nobody likes it but it's revived, it comes back, hangs in there, or people like a movie that later seems to be superficial, and it doesn't seem to work. So I just wonder if time sometimes changes the way we look at literature or any kind of art?
GS: I think that is the case that some books have to mature in their public recognition. Um, it's funny. I was talking to my editor at Poseidon Press Pocket Books who was making the same point as you've just made. There are a number of books which are now quite successful, which if you look back to the year they were published, really made no impression at all and the figures are very low. And yet, over a few years, they break through as quite important books, and I think, arguably, that happens; and the likelihood of that continuing and a permanent place for that book is stronger rather more than those sort of overnight success kind of books, which then are forgotten.

DS: By the same token, books are very ephemeral and very perishable. You cannot walk into the bookstore and expect to find anything you want. Bookstores are highly selective in what they stock. And if you are looking for, sometimes I will read a writer, enchanted by the writer, and want to find the earlier work.
GS: You just can't find it. Right, right.

DS: Search and can't find even anything else in print. Well, I could continue to talk to you on and on. You have given me thirty minutes of your time, and I really appreciate it. I am delighted to have been introduced by Pocket Books to your work, and I'm looking forward to working on this piece because I'd like to see a substantial American audience for it.

GS: Thank you. Thank you.

DS: I certainly wish you the best and I hope you have a nice safe visit here in New York. Maybe you'll get out to New Jersey before you leave.

GS: Well, I'm going on to Boston in fact. I'm going up there for three days before I go back to London, so I will see another American city.

DS: Boston is kind of like New York but it's a lot smaller, slower, but it's a nice town. I think you'll like it.

Graham Swift

Patrick McGrath / 1986

This interview, *Graham Swift by Patrick McGrath*, was commissioned by and first published in BOMB No. 15, Spring 1986. © Bomb Magazine, New Art Publications, and its Contributors. All rights reserved. The BOMB Digital Archive can be viewed at www.bombmagazine.org.

Waterland, first published in England in 1983, immediately established Swift as one of the more original, elegant, and imaginatively fertile of the younger English writers. I recently talked to him about his work in a cold house off the Fulham Road.

Patrick McGrath: You make the point in *Waterland* that history moves in circles, or even spirals, our disasters worsening every time round. Have you been accused of fatalism?

Graham Swift: Not in any deeply offensive way. I tend to shrug that off anyway because novels aren't statements, they aren't prophecies or philosophies, they're stories, and there is a great deal more going on in the novel than simply speculation about the fate of the world. I wouldn't be a novelist if I wanted to be a philosopher, and I hope that what my novels give readers is an experience, not something from which they can extract messages. I rather shudder at the idea. I also ought to say that, bluntly, I don't actually say those things. You can call this sophistical if you like, but it's my character who says these things, it is Tom Crick who holds these views, and he says many things, he says contradictory things; he's a highly intelligent man but he is in a state of personal crisis and his once-cherished and fairly coherent views of history are being challenged, and so he's voicing in the novel different views of history, of progress, the fate of mankind and so on.

PM: Yet Tom Crick carries moral authority in the novel. It is he who speaks, it is he who controls the narrative.

GS: He does exercise a great deal of authority. There is a tendency, I suppose, to take what he says as the last word on things, but against that there is the plight of this man who is heartbroken and reduced and lonely. And what becomes of this man? What becomes of Tom Crick? I think he's a very sad, a very desolate figure, for all his intellectual powers.

PM: Tom Crick's half-brother Dick is a fascinating figure. He is inarticulate and retarded, it's implied that he's half-machine, that he's half-fish, half-eel, even half-vegetable, a potato-head; and he works with silt, which is another of those half-and-half things, water and land; and it's into the silt that he makes his final dive.

GS: I'm not sure that I know, and if I did I wouldn't say, what happens to him at the end. When he dives into the river, you could interpret that as an act of despair, a return to nothingness and soon, but it is also, I hope, a sort of escape, so there is some sort of feeling of liberation. I am, it would seem, interested in inarticulate characters, characters who become silent, inert, vegetable. I think it may have to do with this question of whether knowledge is good or bad: is it good to know the truth, or is it harmful? Are there situations where it's best not to tell, or not to know? Or not to remember? Dick Crick is a character who among his many *semi* attributes has an ability not to remember. He lives in an amnesiac world, and whilst we pity him in some ways, can we be sure that because of this faculty, or nonfaculty, he's not better off than we are? Henry, his grandfather, goes off to fight in the trenches and comes back without a memory: there's a great deal of irony in the book about recalling things or not recalling things. History is constantly confronting this basic choice: why should we summon up the past? Why should we remember anything, whether it's personally or collectively? Does it do us any good? Does it hinder us? And I don't attempt to come down on one side or the other, to resolve the issue, but I suppose you could say that Dick is a peculiar embodiment, among many other things, of this paradox.

PM: What is this thing beneath language that Dick has access to?

GS: I'm not sure that I know. It could simply be nature. Dick seems to be much more part of primitive nature and its primitive cycles than any of the other characters in the book, yet after all human nature does stand apart from nature, and I wouldn't want for one moment to share in that romantic view that going back to nature is a good thing. On the other hand, a complete loss of contact with nature—an inability to see that human nature, even if it is a peculiar and separate phenomenon, is after all a part of nature—is I'm quite sure a bad thing.

PM: Nature at its wildest, the old, wild Fens, provides the setting for one of *Waterland*'s most horrific scenes: the abortion that Martha Clay, an alleged witch, performs on Mary Metcalf. It is evil, and results in septicemia and barrenness for Mary. Yet Martha Clay is as close to nature as Dick Crick.

GS: The reactions I've had to that chapter have been interesting. It is a horrible scene, some people find it almost impossible to read. I've never felt that. I was very conscious of wanting to construct a scene that was very sinister, strong but with a fairytale feeling, for it incorporates so many almost supernatural things. Even for Mary and Tom, the only way they can see it is as something out of a fairytale, in the gruesome sense of fairytale. And I suppose there is no sense of there being any positive outcome. Given that Tom and Mary do want to get rid of the child, one could imagine an outcome where the abortion is successful, if any abortion is; but from the beginning you do have the sense that everything is going to go wrong. Oh, without a doubt it is a central episode in the book.

PM: Is the nature which Martha Clay, the alleged witch, inhabits, the nature to which Dick Crick is connected in his inarticulacy?

GS: I would be reluctant to make these schemes, but if Dick somehow has this contact with nature which the other characters don't have, I wouldn't put Martha Clay in the same category. Her realm is superstition rather than nature, and there's a great deal in the novel about superstition and its vices and virtues. And like many other things in the novel, superstition is paradoxical. I tend to have a paradoxical outlook, I see things in terms of paradox. Superstition, when it creates an event like the abortion scene, is undoubtedly a bad thing. All the potions and the sheer crudeness, the unmedical nature of it all, this has disastrous consequences. But in another sense, in other areas of the novel, superstition, in terms of a need for something extra, is a benign thing. Even telling stories is a kind of superstition, an imposing of extra structure on reality, and it's something very much needed by these people who happen to live in a landscape which almost says to them, look, reality is flat and empty. And all you can do in life is make something, and insofar as superstition is creative, it's perhaps no bad thing.

PM: How was the idea of *Waterland* born?

GS: I think I started with the scene that opens the book, with a picture in my head of the corpse in the river, the floating corpse, and then certain things started to emerge around that, to do with location, setting, other characters, time. So it began as a kind of detective thing, classic case of a dead body, a "whodunit"? The other crucial moment in the gestation was when, having evolved the narrator figure as the boy who lived in the lockside cottage—one of the people who discovers the dead boy—I felt for some reason that this was back in the '40s, in wartime. But I wanted it to be seen and told from a much later perspective, the 1980s. So the question is, naturally, what becomes of this boy Tom in later life? Then, when I made him a history teacher, there was a little—not so little—explosion of ideas. I thought of all sorts of possibilities, all sorts of things that I could bring in, which was very exciting. I think that is when I said, "Well, all right, it is a novel and I can now start it." But we're talking about a process which maybe went on for a year before words got put down on paper.

PM: At what point did you decide to include a natural history of eels?

GS: Well, there's always a large element of serendipity, and also, even though we're talking quite seriously about the book, there is an element of fun. One does have fun when one is writing, although the issues at stake may be very grave. The construction of a novel can be enormous fun. I knew about eels. I didn't know as much as that chapter makes clear, but knew a fair bit about the eels before I started writing *Waterland*. Because I'm a fisherman, I like fishing, I know a bit about fish. Eels have always fascinated me. An incredible lifecycle they have—the mystery of it!—and the extraordinary pseudoscience through the centuries, trying to find out how the damn thing breeds. And I thought, well, this is a wonderful little story in its own right and wouldn't it be great to have the opportunity to sort of just fling it into the middle of some larger work? And the opportunity arose. I found generally that in writing the book I evolved a sort of form, or non-form, in which I could be totally digressive, I could have chapters in which the subject matter was virtually nonfiction, was no longer narrative; and the eel fit superbly into that scheme, because after all the Fens are a region which abounds with eels. The eel has always had metaphorical overtones, like the landscape. And it suddenly seemed to me that the lifecycle, the natural history of the eel, seemed to say so much about history generally, and about our attempts to discover the origin of things, and so on. And all of that was quite apart from it being just an incredibly intriguing and amusing subject.

PM: You mentioned that *Waterland* was much more ambitious than anything you'd attempted before. Were you referring to this integrating of non-narrative, non-fictional material into the story?

GS: Yes, I think that was part of it. I suppose, too, I rather relished in anticipation a slight perplexity on the part of the reader—where the reader comes to the end of one chapter, and then finds a chapter about eels or beer or something, apparently not connected to the narrative. The reader would think, "Well, what the hell's going on." I rather delighted in that prospect.

PM: Will you do it again?

GS: I don't know. I think every book dictates (somehow mysteriously) its own terms. It says to you, well, you can get away with that or you can't. And in any case, it's never a good policy to repeat a pattern.

PM: Do you think it's all right for middle-aged men to run off with small female antelopes?

GS: Well, they don't.

PM: Uncle Walter did.

GS: It was all right for him. I might be wrong in saying they don't. There might be a case somewhere. I'm very fond of that story, I suppose because of the antelope. It was a fairly early story, a story which wrote itself. One invents totally unknown, totally specious species, and that's just good fun.

PM: There's another story in *Learning to Swim*, "The Hypochondriac," in which a doctor projects his clinical knowledge onto a young man, unaware that he's also projecting his own denial of pain; and then to his immense surprise the young man dies. There's a failure of medical knowledge, of scientific thought.

GS: It's a concern which is not unrelated to this business of, "Is it better to know or not to know." It's an illusion that knowledge is always coupled to authority. Knowledge doesn't bring authority, and authority doesn't necessarily imply knowledge. The doctor in that story is a good example of someone who feels that they have knowledge, and indeed they do, but of a very limited kind, in fact. The crisis of that story is really a man's discovery that he has no authority; neither over people, nor, as he once thought, over his own experience, over his own life. There's a great deal in the story about how he's dealt with his own marriage, in terms of "I know what I'm doing, I can deal with this, my knowledge and my clinical cool will hold things together." But it is blown apart, by an incidence of the supernatural, because the patient, who is the cause of all this, who does die, reappears for one moment. Of course, such an event is quite outside the doctor's range of experience. And he breaks down.

PM: It's a lovely delicate ghost, a Jamesian ghost. It just flickers for a moment.
GS: Not really a haunting at all.

PM: Ghosts appear here and there in the short stories, and there's an important ghost, Sarah Atkinson's, in *Waterland*. Yet the earlier novels manifest no such magical or supernatural elements. Why is this?
GS: They were there inside waiting to get out, and they did in *Waterland*. But it's very hard to talk about the construction of a novel in terms of actual decisions to do this or that. Sarah does become a ghost, she returns supernaturally and she dives, as Dick dives; she returns to the water. She began as a solid, flesh-and-blood character who was the young wife of this very solid commercial man, and then I got to the situation where she's knocked unconscious, literally senseless, and remains so.

PM: She hits her head on a writing desk.
GS: Yes, falls and knocks her head against a desk. I see no significance in the writing desk. [laughter] She is another inarticulate character and for the remainder of her life she says virtually nothing. It's as though she passes into ghostliness, almost within her own lifetime, because the people in the town turn her into this curious, angelic, saintly figure, who is invested with strange powers, or so they believe. Then when she dies, almost inevitably you know she's going to come back, she's going to continue to have an influence. But I don't think there was ever a moment when, before writing, I said, well, this is what the character is going to do. You just see possibilities. Some of them you pursue, and you fall flat on your face. Sometimes the pursuit is fruitful.

PM: Two of the observers of Dick Crick's plunge into the silt are American servicemen. It's sunset. Overhead, bombers are flying off to their targets. Is this an implication of Americans in some final apocalyptic moment, in some sort of global plunge?
GS: No, I haven't seen it that way, but I don't see why you shouldn't. I thought you were going to say, can you use the presence of the Americans

in some way to indicate a sort of New World—Americans from the New World who have come into this old and in some ways inbred and failing English world. There was possibly an element of that. And I don't suppose I chose entirely by accident the state where these Americans came from: Arizona, the dry zone; and there they are in the wet Fens. One mustn't forget too that historically it's quite accurate, there were many American servicemen based in East Anglia at that time.

PM: Do you really see Dick Crick as an individual?

GS: Very much so, very much the character fiddling with his motorbike. I don't see him as a sort of cipher, symbol, representation—he's certainly very there. Some of the little things he keeps in his bedside cupboard . . .

PM: A bird's nest?

GS: Oh, he has little bits of animal skulls, and a pathetic sort of thing he made out of a tin for his mother on one of her birthdays.

PM: There's a fish hanging over the bed.

GS: A stuffed pike, which is quite important in the story. I do like the concrete. Novels should be this mixture of the intensely concrete and the world of ideas.

PM: Many stories are told in *Waterland*, and one of the funniest is the story of Jack Parr's suicide attempt. Jack is a railway signalman, and decides to end it all by sitting on the railway lines. So he sits there doggedly all night, while unbeknownst to him his wife is up in the signal box, throwing switches and making telephone calls, and lights are blinking all over the eastern Fens as expresses and goods trains are rerouted to avoid the unhappy man.

GS: He's asleep by this time, and he never learns about the subterfuge. And is actually convinced when he wakes up that he's been saved by a miracle. And nobody breaks this illusion.

PM: He goes on the wagon and stays on it. Many events in *Waterland* are seen to have two explanations, often one logical, the other superstitious. A live fish dropped into a woman's lap will make her barren, it's said; and this is precisely what does happen to Mary.

GS: Yes, you can imagine some of the old people in the Fens maintaining staunchly that the reason for all the trouble was the eel, the fish in the lap. There's a parallel in some ways between superstition and the way fiction works, the way fiction can produce these rather magical moments, which aren't entirely impossible, aren't entirely beyond belief. I think it's important for fiction to be magical, just as it's important for fiction to embrace the real world, to look really hard at the real world.

PM: Real world?

GS: Whatever the real world is.

PM: Now, this feeling for magic is quite new to the English novel.

GS: Yes, that's true, it's not at all a recognizable English tradition. The phrase everybody comes up with is "magical realism," which I think has now become a little tired. But on the other hand there's no doubt that English writers of my generation have been very much influenced by writers from outside who in one way or another have got this magical, surreal quality, such as Borges, Márquez, Grass, and that that has been stimulating. I think in general it's been a good thing. Because we are, as ever, terribly parochial, self-absorbed, and isolated, culturally, in this country. It's about time we began to absorb things from outside.

PM: What about France?

GS: I think there's always been a cultural antagonism between us and the French, but I think also the French may have held the view, and justifiably so, that English fiction of the immediate postwar period, up to the '60s and earlier '70s, was terribly bound up in its own Englishness, middle-class suburbs and so forth, and that it just didn't travel. But they're more interested now in English writers than they used to be.

PM: Have they warmed to *Waterland*?

GS: Quite. I was asked to go over there, be around for a few days and so on. It was entered for some prize they have for novels in translation. It was shortlisted but it didn't win.

PM: Who amongst your contemporaries do you particularly enjoy?

GS: Well, I actually like very much a writer who's originally American, Russell Hoban, who wrote *Riddley Walker*. He seems to me to be completely his own man as a writer. I think he's got a real touch of genius. Then there's a writer who's originally Japanese, Kazuo Ishiguro, and he's about to publish a second novel. His first was called *A Pale View of Hills*, and it is simply amazing. He's a remarkable writer in an understated, very quiet, unextrovert way. There's Timothy Mo, who is also about to publish a new book. His second novel was called *Sour Sweet*, which is a lovely book about the Chinese community in London. Some of these writers I know quite well as friends. One of the pleasures of having written a successful book is that you do get more opportunity to meet other writers. For a long time, really till *Waterland*, I knew virtually no other writers. Not that it changed anything fundamentally. In some ways you can argue that knowing other writers is a disruption, a distraction. You can become more concerned about how other people write, which is not necessarily good for your own work. I think in the end writing is a lonesome business. You have to go away by yourself to do it, whether you've got hundreds of friends or not. Nothing will ever change that.

PM: Would you like a glass of beer?
GS: Yes please.

PM: There's a book by a French writer, Michel Tournier, which I think might be to your taste. It's called *Friday, or The Other Island*, and it's a sort of postcolonial rewrite of *Robinson Crusoe*. The relationship of Crusoe and Friday grows increasingly uneasy—Friday blows up the gunpowder supply and runs away—and Robinson becomes increasingly distraught. His one solace is a peaceful little patch of ground in a very obscure part of the island, which he becomes closer and closer to, this patch of black earth, until finally he's regularly inseminating it, he's making love to the earth. Then, to his delight, he begins to see these beautiful white flowers appear—he has successfully inseminated the earth! And as things get worse and worse with Friday, so Robinson comes to spend more and more time in his secret place. Till one day he goes up, and there amongst his white flowers, is a *black* flower—and this is a major crisis—and things go from bad to worse.

Interview with Graham Swift

Marc Porée / 1993

Originally published in La Quinzaine *littéraire* (1993) 621: 10–11. Reprinted by permission of *Nouvelle Quinzaine littéraire*. Translated from the French by Dori St. Amant.

Marc Porée: The strength of your novels comes from orchestrating the collapse of a certain number of false ideas, of erroneous concepts, on which your characters based their lives, and which collapse in silence, without the world around them feeling the traces of this profound shock—"This Consciousness that is aware"—in the words of Emily Dickinson.

Graham Swift: Yes, I am also thinking of Bruegel's painting, which represents the fall of Icarus, in one corner of the painting, and the absence of consequences on the rhythm of days going by in the foreground. It's cruel, but it's so true. My narrators are still in a state of crisis, of catastrophe. This is what triggers in them and in me the desire and the need for the story. It is the only valid motivation in my eyes. My subjects often come to me, following a strange event, the discovery, for example, what we take for granted, in the real world, or in our beliefs, is abruptly placed in a new light, unfamiliar. This is how the Darwinian revolution, which is at the heart of *Ever After*, was all the more traumatic in its implications because it destroyed an "illusion," shattered the appearance of a theocentric vision of the world, creating a new kind of "reality."

That said, at the risk of appearing paradoxical, it is only very slowly that Darwin appears in the novel. Initially, I was not drawn in by his presence, as a character in any case, but he eventually prevailed. To me, the real question is less what he did and more why it was Darwin, and not another. Nothing seemed to predispose him to this kind of discovery. In essence, what I'm passionate about is the exploration through writing: to solve the mystery in and around personality—at any given moment, a seemingly ordinary character sees his life dramatically turn upside down.

MP: Where does this astonishing maturity come from—these meanings so sure of the gravitas—which leads you to choose characters-narrators often much older than you?

GS: They have to put forward a treasure of accumulated experience as well as their place in history. And then, you know, I get a little closer to them every day. The time will come when I, having reached this age, will turn—who knows?—to teenage characters . . . if only to find this distance from my subject, to which I am very attached as a novelist.

MP: What about the contentious relationships that children—often sons—have with their parents—often their fathers—in your novels?

GS: There is nothing personal to see here in any case. Again, it is the distance from my own life, normally harmonious on this level, that motivates me. Inventing what I did not know. That said, I must confess to you that the year I finished this book about death, my father died. This is disturbing to say the least . . .

MP: The fact that your fathers are often spies—that's true of *Shuttlecock*, as well as in the case of *Bill Unwin's Father* . . .

GS: A must see with the game of illusion and reality. They are also soldiers, authority figures in a word (see *Out of This World*). I was born not long after the end of the Second World War, and my novels bear the mark of these glorious myths that stirred around me, in the '50s, the years of my childhood. It has come back to us novelists to shatter these myths.

MP: And then, there is the father figure of Hamlet, of whom you make such a rich use, intertextuality—you'd have to say the Shakespearian "bitextuality" plays in full force in *Ever After*.

GS: That's evident. But the quote that seems central to me is that stated by Hamlet's mother when she asks him, "Why seems it so particular with thee?" Why would anything matter, after all? The fact, particular, stubborn, resolute, that they have, that is what interests me. Bill Unwin takes things very much to heart. What I also do as a writer. But I also share—the virtue of doubling—the astonishment of Hamlet's mother.

MP: And if I proposed to define the Anglicite—a universal vocation—from your novel, by its implicit reference to this other quote from Shakespeare: "all the world's a stage"?

GS: In fact, the idea that the world is only a scene where representations play out appeals to me a lot, and I see something profoundly liberating for the novelist. To think that we all populate a theater of shadows, far from being a hindrance, on the contrary, creates, for me, an opening. I see the major philosophical questioning as touching the uncertain status of reality. *Ever After*, more than any other of my novels, perhaps, is steeped with this question. The nagging question returns: What constitutes the identity of a person—of an actress, for example—her mystery, her degree of "reality"? Finally, more broadly, love does not tolerate the close examination of the realist—and yet, love, this hollow thing, romantic, is instinctive.

MP: Your language is partly responsible for the "Swift Effect." It is so close to the poetry that saturates and surrounds it, that I want to ask you who your favorite poets are.
GS: Keats, mainly for the great Odes. The Elizabethan and Jacobean poetry, which intervene massively in the novel. Shakespeare, too, of course, the greatest of all. At the risk of appearing a bit chauvinistic, I would say that he is such a great poet that you can skip reading the others.

MP: One also has the impression, in this geological novel, that you went looking for words to carve in them, at the bottom of the mine, like a precious mineral. You must devote considerable energy to this work?
GS: That's right. Critics often say that I write too slowly. I tell them that I'm going at my own pace. A novel takes me from three to four years. I recognize that I am a demanding writer on the choice of words, often laborious in the process. I come back to the task, nothing is really easy. At the risk of being a little pretentious, I would say that every phrase, every word, counts. I like being able to say of a book that I just finished, that one cannot change a word without altering the whole. That may not be true, but that's what I believe. This puts me in a situation of extreme responsibility—still a heavy Victorian virtue to bear—in relation to the construction of the novel.

MP: I would indeed say that you bring words to their peak, of maximum tension—their breaking point, almost. And after all this entire novel is a novel of ruptures . . . But it's also a novel where you take risks. Like, for example, calling your character . . . Unwin. Do you think you overdo the onomastics of failure, of pathos?
GS: If it were to be redone, I would not do it again.

MP: Another risk. Your novel talks about mortality, expresses the pre-sentiments of mortality—but also, of course, immortality. It does it with a poignant gravity. But also at the price of a macabre fixation on the "serial" disappearance of your characters, that you make disappear, one after the other, almost.

GS: To give you a "realistic" answer I would say that families hit by a series of deaths, I know, is nothing exceptional or implausible. And then, it is the same reproach that can be directed at plays like *Hamlet*, as well as many other tragedies. This is part of, I believe, the conventions of literature.

MP: Last risk, perhaps. What happened to the perversity that was of interest in *Shuttlecock*, your last novel translated into French, with which *Ever After* bears a certain resemblance? Why such a sentimental romance this time?

GS: For me, there is nothing pejorative in this word that often covers something deeper. I claim to be sentimental. Literature is just that—the work of emotion. And then, irony is never far away.

An Interview with Graham Swift

Catherine Bernard / 1995

Originally published in *Contemporary Literature* 38.2 (1997): 216–231. ©1997 by the Board of Regents of the University of Wisconsin System. Reprinted by permission of the University of Wisconsin Press.

Graham Swift was born in 1949 in London. His has been the fairly straightforward path of someone devoted to fiction, whose studies at Cambridge, then York logically led to writing, although he spent some ten years teaching and writing in London and Greece before his first novel—*The Sweet-Shop Owner* (1980)—was published. The main themes to be taken up and developed in the novels that followed, and in his collection of short stories (*Learning to Swim*, 1982), are all to be found in this low-key, subdued text, this tale of dereliction and deception, of remorse and pain, in which the protagonists are gradually invaded by an excruciating feeling of private and historical inadequacy.

Whether they be in direct contact with history, as is the case of Harry Beech, the war photographer of *Out of This World* (1988), or allotted the ambiguous tasks of indexing and classifying it (*Shuttlecock*, 1981), or interpreting it, as is the case of Tom Crick, the history teacher of *Waterland* (1983), Swift's narrators experience a breakdown, a dislocation of the political and social body: private and collective destinies no longer coincide. *Last Orders* (1996), which came out two months after this interview was conducted, takes this theme to its breaking point. In this polyphonic novel, the characters seem to be left stranded on the wayside of history, to contend with their disintegrating dreams of self-adequacy, with haunting memories of betrayal and failure.

History is but a "thin garment," or so Tom Crick suggests in *Waterland*, a garment pieced together from the tatters of private experience and worn threadbare by time and disillusion. Relentlessly, from the private tragedy exhumed in *The Sweet-Shop Owner*, or in *Last Orders*, to the philosophical doubts of *Ever After* (1992), which focuses on the epistemological revolution caused by Darwinism, Swift means to come to terms with the increasing inorganicity of historical destiny.

Swift's handling of the realist legacy is, in that respect, a highly subversive and paradoxical one. His is an anxious, dissident form of realistic representation that—as Swift himself insists in this interview—still subscribes to the cognitive agenda of fictional representation, while acknowledging the need to evolve narrative forms flexible enough to be endowed with a renewed reliability and relevance. Polyphony is but one of the strategies used in *Out of This World, Ever After*, and *Last Orders*, allowing Swift to explore the multiplicity of reality, of the "here and now," and the intrinsically paradoxical nature of history, but above all the human fiction-making impulse.

For Swift, man is "the story-making animal," an "amphibious" animal (a metaphor inspired, perhaps, by Swift's passion for fishing) which for all its capacity for survival in a hostile reality yearns to return to its natural element: myth, fiction. Stories are more than placating stratagems to face reality; they inform it, are given a hermeneutic function. Hence in his novels, the constant confrontation of our fabulating capacities with the harshest of realities: death, loss, madness, suffering, oblivion. Hence also the jubilation that lies for all the narrators in endlessly retrieving the past by rewriting it, by telling it anew. Hence finally the proliferating logic of the narrative texture.

Swift's novels proceed via endless analogies, metaphorical associations, connotations which bring fact and vision into an organic whole. In *Waterland*, the reclamation of land in East Anglia becomes metaphorical of remembrance and of the textual logic itself, since the text moves forward by retrieving and modulating themes and images that slowly become obsessive. In *Last Orders*, a day trip embarked upon to commemorate the death of a friend turns out to be metaphorical of the painful work of mourning that the characters' lives have become.

Like his characters, Swift revels in "spinning yarns," revels too in the dappled vividness of language, in its energy, as the vernacular of *Last Orders* testifies. His latest novel should also be read as homage to the resilience of the community spirit of certain working-class districts of the capital, where Swift has lived for many years. He is a devoted Londoner, as is evident in many of his novels, and it was in one of his favorite restaurants in Kensington that we met for this interview, on 1 November 1995. The special quality of the changing autumn light on the dark brick walls of Kensington was our first topic of conversation. Swift's intensity and concentration cannot be adequately conveyed on paper. He is as careful in the analysis of his private commitment to fiction as he can be in the choice of an adjective, as wary of any form of pigeonholing as he is of ostentation and insincerity.

Q: I want to start with a question about the place of voice in your novels, because it has always seemed to me that you create voices more than characters. How do you see the role of voice in your novels?

A: It is a wonderful question to start with, very apropos. I can't help thinking about my new novel, in which voice is terribly important—whatever the exact definition of voice in a novel is, because I don't think that voice in a novel is like the voice people talk in. However much I draw on that sense of things, literary voices are very specific and sophisticated things. You have got to gauge it very carefully. Voice is important because, as you know, I tend to write in the first person, which immediately implies voice, even if that voice is internal and is the voice of someone talking to themselves, within themselves, and perhaps in a way that they wouldn't in any other circumstances talk. I think that a lot of the business I am terribly anxious about, the vital business of finding your way into the novel, is finding the voice. You may have a character, you may have a sense of the character and a situation and a story, but until you find a voice, you can't really begin; and sometimes, when you give up on a novel, it is exactly for that reason, because the voice is wrong. All of this means that there is a sort of inner ear, which I think I have quite well tuned, and I hope my reader does too, because I think the actual act of reading is to do with using an inner ear, and that is why reading aloud from a novel is sometimes a rather odd experience, because it's then you realize that though you can read aloud from a novel, you are in fact writing for this inner ear, this silent listening.

Q: Could we push the metaphor even further and say that it has got something to do with music, that somehow a novel can be akin to a sort of musical score?

A: I would agree with that. I am not sure how to place voice—I don't necessarily think of the voice in a novel in a musical way. But I would certainly think of structure, I would think of other things—things not to do with persons and character—as musical, as having to do with pace and rhythm in the same way as music. Again, finding your way into a novel with that underlying music is vital.

Q: And yet, to come back to the problem of voice, it seems as well that the narrators especially are somehow also theatrical masks; they put on this voice, probably to conceal something.

A: It may not be their real voice. It is the voice they use; it is the voice that is recognizable to them, which is habitual perhaps, but it may not be their true voice. I mean, that is full of potential for the narrative, because then you can show or suggest a breakdown of voice which may or may not reveal some underlying voice, a deeper voice. There are levels of voices. Often the superficial voice can be quite forced; it may be the voice of the front that they put before the world, which can be destroyed by a crisis in their life. And often that is a starting point for the story, for the narrators' telling.

Q: It seems that so much of the intensity of your novels depends on this pitch and also—I am thinking of *Ever After* and *Waterland*—on the saturation of the text with repetitions, analogies. You were talking of rhythm and pace; do you think that these two elements are linked, the saturation of the voice and the saturation of the repetitive texture of the novel?

A: I think that repetition can be a structural thing; it can be echo, reminder. When you think of it in terms of voice, the things that people ordinarily choose to repeat are quite telling. Why do some people stress and repeat certain things rather than others? They are often suggestions of things going on underneath. I think I explore such things. Possibly I have become less repetitious in a formal, structural sense; *Waterland* was full of very deliberate repetitions. I think I now avoid that. I am skeptical of that.

Q: Why skeptical?

A: I think I want more and more to be simple. I want to do less to achieve more, which dramatically implies that you shouldn't repeat yourself. I think that there was a degree of overemphasis in *Waterland*, and if I can be self-critical, it's possible that because it was a long time ago, *Waterland* contained perhaps a little too much repetition, an underscoring of things, excessive emphasis. If I were writing it now, which of course I am not and I never would, I would probably go about it in a different way. It is not to disown it in any way, far from it. I recognize that over a period of more than fifteen years, your approach to writing does change, does crystallize.

Q: Would you say that what has changed is the way you instill intensity in the text? You were saying that *Waterland* was possibly overdone. I disagree . . .

A: Well, there is another way of looking at it which is more generous to myself, which is simply that *Waterland* was the kind of novel it was—a legitimate kind of novel. There are other kinds of novels which I am more interested in now.

Q: Because it seems that on the contrary in *Shuttlecock* and *Ever After* what matters is the crystallization of tension at certain moments or even in certain words. I am thinking of your use of adjectives in *Ever After*, such as "divine." So could we say that your handling of emphasis has shifted?

A: One purpose of repetition in any novel is to create a kind of language which is specific to that novel. It creates the general language within which certain words, phrases, linguistic ideas are going to be specific to the world of your novel. And they are like a separate language. You build that up partly by a process of repetition, by saying, "remember this word, because in this world, in this area of language, it is going to be special." I think that is what all novelists do, consciously or not. I am quite conscious of its happening, of the way a relatively ordinary, innocent adjective can have within the context of a novel almost a new meaning. That's an exciting thing to achieve.

Q: It also has a new meaning depending on the moment it occurs in the text.

A: You can store up the potential of a word or a phrase which is specific to the novel for a certain point where it might have a maximum effect. Again, I think I am quite conscious of doing this. It can be quite powerful.

Q: In *Ever After* there is that wonderful moment when the mother and the child are eating pears. It is really a climactic episode which is concentrated, distilled in that word "divine" which, among other things, has strong erotic overtones at that precise moment.

A: Well, that word "divine" is one of the most untranslatable things, I would say, because whatever else that word is doing, whatever other meaning has been invested in that word, it is a word which—to come back to voice—when spoken, in an English voice, by certain English people—I say certain English people, because not everyone would use that word, far from it—but that word "divine" used—without any thought of its real meaning to do with divinity—to express pleasure, to express delight, is very much something which you will hear. It is fraught with all kinds of social associations.

Q: Would you say that you play with the original meaning of the word and its discrepant social, emotional, and textual relevance?

A: Yes, because in that context it conveys at least four or five things. It conveys something about the character of the mother, very strongly so. It conveys an erotic charge which the boy registers for the first time and holds on to. He remembers it. It has both generally and in terms of the novel a complex sense of things being divine, God-given, wonderful, an idea which is partly related to the whole argument about Darwin and religion. But also I think, in a more general sense, there are certain moments, certain experiences in life where you feel that something extraneous to normal existence has occurred, and it has to be registered in words like "divine," which are used by unreligious people to register something that is almost religious.

Q: I would like to move to a question about the place of the literary heritage in your work, in the physical meaning of the term "place," if one thinks of *Ever After*, and about the way contemporary writing and literary tradition are related and at the same time alien. How do you incorporate literary tradition in your texts?

A: No matter how consciously or not I deal with it or demonstrate it, I have a very strong sense of tradition, because of having had quite a thorough education in English literature. Now how does that actually affect my writing? I think whatever else I do specifically, it does give me confidence, strength in a sense that I don't think every writer would understand. It is almost as though merely to know that there is a tradition somehow out of which I have come is a very comforting and strengthening and confidence-giving thing. But to be more specific, yes, in certain things I have written I have quite deliberately referred to, exploited, used, even mimicked an English literary tradition, although not in a backward-looking approach to things, but because there is still a place for that within a contemporary way of writing. I think it is hard to separate the literary tradition from the language. If you use the English language, you are using a language which has so many literary overtones, which connects you to English places, English culture. And as a Londoner, writing in English, sometimes about London, and it is particularly so in my latest novel, you know that you are drawing on this sort of literary blood that is still flowing. I recognize it more than others. Whether you recognize it or not, it is there.

Q: Does that explain the importance of the inheritance motif in your novels? Because one of the main themes of your work is heritage, whether it be family inheritance, historical heritage . . .

A: Clearly that involves a feeling for tradition of that certain kind. I would say that it is not related to literary tradition, but it may be. It is an area where other people might know best. What that immediately relates to for me is simply a strong sense of historical connections, connections through the generations, which aren't necessarily to do with tradition. This sense can have something to do with the opposite, with going against the grain, with going against the received notions, against the received pattern, and this sense of contradictory connection is something I have got as much time for as for tradition. Sometimes you actually have to be antitradition.

Q: You sometimes insist on the moral quality of the sense of finality in your novels. Would you define yourself as a moralist—that is, as a writer who tries to come to terms with the moral pressures bearing on people?
A: I don't think I am. The word "moralist" suggests to me someone of a nonnovelistic frame of mind—a social analyst, a philosopher, rather than a novelist. I don't think I would be at all happy to have that label put upon me. On the other hand, I do think that what I do is deeply moral, if only for the simple reason that all morality, all real morality, rests on doing what a novelist makes a specialty of—that is, attempting to get inside the experience of others, and unless you do that . . . I would be at a loss to know where true moral feelings come from without that. So I think that whatever else novels do, and they may be doing many things, they do fulfill a highly moral function. It is not one that people would identify as moral, if their notion of morality is something which can be reduced to rules and discipline, but it is nevertheless the basis of morality. Imagination is the basis of morality.

Q: So would writing, morality, and empathy be related?
A: Yes, because empathy is the beginning of sympathy, sympathy is the beginning of compassion, and compassion is where morality really accrues. Empathy really goes without saying. If as a novelist you are not in the business of empathy, then what are you doing? The word "empathy" in English is fairly neutral. You can have empathy without sympathy. They are different things. In the end, empathy is the more basic of the two. That's just an ability to get a flavor, a little sort of vibration of what someone else experiences. To get out of yourself is empathy. It might lead on to better and greater things.

Q: Could that explain why the two main literary shadows in your texts are Charles Dickens and George Eliot?

A: They may no longer be. I get very worried about declarations of influence, for a variety of reasons. One is that, again, over time, whatever your influences may have been and whatever you may have felt them to have been at a particular time, they do change. Maybe they don't matter so much as they once did. I have said myself that Dickens has been an influence on my writing, and on top of that, because it has been discovered that I once did a portion of a doctorate on Dickens, people have extrapolated from that, perhaps unfairly. I wouldn't reject that Dickens is a writer I have read with huge attention, that he is a force. But I would hesitate to talk about Dickens and George Eliot as ghosts in my writing.

Q: To me it has got something to do precisely with the link between language and a sense of place and also with what you have just been saying about empathy, sympathy, and writing as modes of experiencing what others feel. It seems that these elements are at the heart of Dickens and Eliot.

A: If you say the nineteenth-century novel must in some way haunt the twentieth-century novel, it becomes almost impossible to find anyone of whom you couldn't say that one or the other or some mixture of the two aren't present in what they are doing, because Dickens and Eliot are two great representative novelists of that century, and they are very different, and it is as though they complement each other because they are different. They are the two halves of the novelistic world, and most writers, even if they haven't read them, share a combination of the forces that are working in them. Dickens was a great novelist of spontaneity and energy, of things which are not necessarily subjective scrutiny, and yet it is the energy going with the humanity which sometimes achieves extraordinarily instinctive and intuitive things. George Eliot was in my view the great intelligence, the great analyst. There is enormous emotional force at work in her novels. But there is above all a desire to go into the forces bearing on man.

Q: It seems that you have been more influenced by the humanist tradition of English fiction than by the more comical, farcical tradition of Sterne, Fielding . . .

A: Yes, you are right, so far, which does not mean that I have no time for that other tradition. Of course I am aware of the evolution of the English novel, but the eighteenth-century novel is not something which obviously appears to affect my work. I think that as an author I have to reserve a lot of judgment, because the thing about influence is that you do not really know who influences you. I find the whole business of having to declare your influences more and more troublesome. It is so tempting to say I am influenced by X simply to get rid of the question. And then people will take you up on this and tell you about it and thereafter you start saying you have indeed been influenced by X. There is a measure of that with the Dickens thing. I do not want to dismiss it, but it has been overplayed a bit.

Q: Would you agree with Malcolm Bradbury's idea, which I find extremely enlightening, that contemporary English writers have incorporated the greater sense of formal awareness of the modernists, but that this awareness is itself counterbalanced by the nineteenth-century novel and its humanist and moral intent, in a sort of retroactive way?
A: I generally would agree with that. I am not sure how it works when you apply it to individual writers. I can apply it to myself fairly comfortably. As I said a moment ago, my sense of tradition is one which, whatever else, does give me confidence, or maybe a better word would be balance. Whatever course you are steering, you are kept on balance by your feeling of tradition. There is the weight of tradition which stops you flying off in all directions. So I think you could make a general point along those lines, that because there is a strong tradition of the English novel, contemporary English writers, consciously or not, are kept under a sort of positive, good restraint by that feeling: "Yes, there was George Eliot, there was Dickens, I am doing something different, but nonetheless it helps that they were there, I would be lost if they hadn't been there."

Q: In other words, the sense of form is counterbalanced by the urge to try to tackle issues which are not exclusively related to form and experimentation.
A: It is a very complicated area, because if you then start to think about the world of the middle of the nineteenth century, if you think of society then—as far as you can—and society now, of course there is a huge difference. And I think some writers who, unlike me, would have a thing about tradition would react by saying, "Of course the world is not like that anymore; people don't even speak like they did anymore"—if, that is, dialogue and conversation in the nineteenth-century novel was a real reflection of the way people spoke at the time. What you hear a lot is, "It is impossible to write a novel now like Dickens and George Eliot did, you've got to do something else." I would agree with that, but what I have never been able to define is exactly why not. There is a kind of intuitive feeling that of course you can't—of course life is not like it was then, so a novel cannot be like it was. But there is some mystery, to be honest, some paradox to it which I don't understand.

Q: Could it have something to do with the difficulty of acknowledging the idea that fiction is, whether we like it or not, somehow referential and determined by its own time? We can't escape the mimetic intent.

A: I honestly don't know. I admit to a lot of confusion about this. I suppose I do have a perhaps quite silly notion that life in the nineteenth century was perhaps more like life as described in a nineteenth-century novel than life in the twentieth century is to life—whatever that is—in a twentieth-century novel. The fact that I hesitate to use the word "life" is almost to suggest that the twentieth-century novel is not about life in an obvious sense. It does not want to look out the window and say, "Well that's what I want to talk about." If it does, you can't write about it in the same way. Obviously, when I am writing, I am not thinking about these things. I reflect on them afterwards. I suspect that George Eliot and Dickens had a sense of form that was quite different from the sense of form a writer might have now. They almost didn't have a sense of form. They did these things on a serial basis, for magazines, and then they were completed, and that's what they were. That was their form. They didn't construct. It would be lovely to have that innocence, that absence of the urge to construct. But for better or worse we are lumbered with it. We are very aware of construction.

Q: And would you say that to some extent you write almost against that urge to construct? The way you address certain painful issues—loss, the presence of the past—seems to contradict the hyperawareness we have of form today, as if you were saying, "Right, we have to go back to the essentials of experience."

A: I think we do. We always do. That's how it works. If you can't do that, something is lacking. Although it's odd; I think I have a very strong sense of form. I know when something is right or wrong; my sense of form stands me in good stead, which might suggest that I am a formalist. But I am absolutely not a formalist, because what does matter to me are things as felt, and feeling seems at least to stand in opposition to form: form is to do with control and discipline, and feeling is to do with liberation and release. And yet I suppose that's a truism about art—you can't have one without the other. I accept that. But there is an awful lot of formalism that is mere artifice; there is an awful lot of mere cleverness with form, and I think we've got to strive to be simple. It's the form which goes unnoticed which is successful. As soon as it draws attention to itself, it just clanks. And it does, in my case, happen to do very much with a sort of musical sense. But you do, in the end, know when something is right. I don't think it's being confident or arrogant. I read a fair amount of contemporary fiction. The thing is, the work might be fiddled with the mechanics of form, but there is no feeling about what form should be giving, a sort of generosity . . .

Q: How can generosity be instilled in form?

A: It can be done. I have my own rather personal literary theory: I tend to divide writers between the defensive and . . . I am not sure if I have a word for the other kind of writer, but it is the kind of writer who isn't a defensive writer. But I think there is an awful lot of writing which in its cleverness, in its insistence on formal virtuosity is only defensive and hiding the writer. Not that it's the work of a novelist to say "Hey, look at me" when he's writing. But diffidence is sometimes hiding even that part the writer has in common with other people and which above all should be exposed. There is a lot of attention given to form and style, a lot of heavy self-consciousness about style, about linguistic expertise, which again I think is defensive and protective. It's like somebody putting on a suit of armor to keep in the things that matter rather than to show them. And then there is the kind of writer who tends not to do that, and how you don't do that, I don't really know, but I hope I am one of those people who doesn't defend. Vulnerability—that's the thing. When you read a novel you get a strong sense sometimes of the authority of the writer—an author ought to have authority; it's in the very word. It's not like someone saying, "I am telling you so." It's not coming down from on high. You think the author knows. It's the authority of some sort of special knowledge. It makes sure that the reader trusts the writer. It's to do with trust. And you say, "I will carry on reading this, because I think I am in good hands with this person." Often all that stems from the realization that the writer is prepared to show that vulnerability. At the same time—again, I don't know how you do achieve this, but I hope I do achieve it—vulnerability and authority are diametrical opposites, but there is some sort of authority which comes from someone saying "Trust me because I am vulnerable." All sorts of things can reinforce that, and I am feeling one of them is form. I am desperate to avoid a sense of the power derived from form. I don't want to say "Look at me being clever!" instead of "Look at me as someone like you!" So I hope I am not a defensive writer.

Q: Could your definition of the necessary vulnerability of the writer be compared to what Virginia Woolf says about the impersonality of the writer? She was highly aware of the possibilities of form; but she also hoped to find a voice that would deprive her of her omnipotent control over her works.

A: Yes, I agree with that. It is not the only route to take. But I think you become undefensive, vulnerable, and the security becomes strong at the same time, when you dispense with yourself, whatever that actually means in terms of a specific novel. It might mean your ability to enter as one hundred percent as this is possible another character: I mean your ability to see the world through somebody else's eyes and not constantly insist on yourself. That is what achieves this happy mixture of both vulnerability and something that is highly to be trusted, a certain sense that as a reader I recognize. There are those defensive writers of whom I am afraid I can say by page thirty, "Oh yes, this is all very clever but very defensive, and it's no good to me," and I put it aside.

Q: Could this have something to do with the very old-fashioned notion of identification which we've been desperately trying to get rid of? Because writing and reading somehow hinge on the concept of identity—the identity of the narrative voice, the identity of the character, the specific identity of style . . .
A: Readers want to identify with the experience of the character; they want to become part of it. Readers don't want to identify with the author; they want to have the feeling that the author's reliability is at work so that they can then get on with the more exciting business of identifying with the story.

Q: So this swapping of identities very much depends on storymaking.
A: It depends absolutely on storiness, which the more I write the more I ought to become jaded about, although I find the opposite is true. The story is the heart of the matter. However you talk about it, however you analyze it, it is this ultimately magical, marvelous, mysterious, wonderful thing. It's got to be there. That's what makes the reader read. Whatever else you're attempting, whatever else you're doing, it's the story that remains. I know it is not a very fashionable view of fiction.

Q: I think we're rediscovering the value of storiness, the more we understand that experience is simply stories. We survive by telling ourselves stories, by fictionalizing our lives.
A: Absolutely. Quite apart from the special domain of novels, in life generally we're constantly telling stories, constantly comforting ourselves, each other, entertaining ourselves and each other, strengthening ourselves and each other through telling narratives of one kind or another; they don't have to be sophisticated.

Q: Meaning-making in a sense is story-making. Storymaking conditions the way we make sense of our lives and the world.

A: Yes, so that it only makes more ridiculous that question writers get asked, "So what is the meaning of your novel?"—because the meaning is the story.

Graham Swift in Interview
On *Last Orders*

Bettina Gossmann et al. / 1997

From *Anglistik: International Journal of English Studies* 8.2 (1997): 155–60.
Reprinted by permission of the publisher and editors of *Anglistik*.

The following interview took place on 17 March 1997 in "Hotel Oper," Düsseldorf. The interviewers were Bettina Gossmann, Roman Haak, Melanie Romberg and Saskia Spindler, a group of students from the Department of English at Düsseldorf University.

Question: Were you inspired by the people you meet in your local pub when creating the characters for *Last Orders*?
Graham Swift: No, I don't think I was inspired in that direct way by people in a pub, if only because I make up my characters. I certainly don't base my characters on people I know personally or on people that I meet or I see. But of course, the characters in the book are very like people you might find in a pub. But I don't think the inspiration came directly from there.

Question: The most notorious German literary critic, Marcel Reich-Ranicki, said about *Last Orders*: "It's brilliantly written, but I don't find the life of common people interesting at all."—What do you think makes the characters in your book interesting?
GS: Well, I think he has a problem. I always wanted to write about so-called ordinary people and ordinary things, if only because I believe there is no such thing as an ordinary person, but everyone is extraordinary, everyone is unique, everyone has something special inside him, and so the challenge of writing about ordinary and common things is to show that. I think that's much more interesting than starting off with obviously exciting or special things, that doesn't appeal to me. What would literature be, if it

did not include a sense of range? You can write about anything. There's no exclusion. That's why I think this man's remarks, as far as I know what they were, were very limited.

Question: Is it because you are a male writer that women don't have much to say in *Last Orders*?
GS: I would disagree with that. They have a lot to say, principally through the voice of Amy, through the widow, who I think is actually the strongest character. And though her voice doesn't emerge till past half-way through the book, I think her voice is the strongest and she has the greatest power of decision in the book. So I would say although obviously on the surface it seems—it's far from being a book just about men in a male world.

Question: Many people have referred to *Last Orders* as a kind of remake of Faulkner's *As I Lay Dying*. Do you feel flattered or offended when you hear that?
GS: It depends what they're saying. Firstly, there's never been a secret about there being an echo of Faulkner in my book. Faulkner is a writer I admire, particularly *As I Lay Dying* which is the book which gets mentioned. If you write about people dealing intimately with the remains of the dead, it will be very hard not to evoke such a classic novel which is also on that subject. But, I mean, having said that, my book is my book. You could equally say that if you write about such a very basic common story, such a timeless story, that it belongs to no writer. It's a story which has to be retold over and over again.

Question: So you rather feel flattered?
GS: Yes, I certainly feel flattered. But it doesn't surprise me, because it is there, in the same way that there is a connection in *Last Orders* with Chaucer, because you have those characters journeying on much the same route. And as they journey their stories come out. There's as much a connection with Chaucer as with Faulkner. The important thing is to say that these connections are just a tiny part of a novel which is mine.

Question: Did you think about Chaucer while you were writing the episode about Canterbury?
GS: Not especially that episode. I think Chaucer was just a figure, and then *The Canterbury Tales* were there at the back of my mind as something that quite obviously was echoed in my modern day story, and such echoes seem

to me to be something which can enrich. You know, those references can enrich, they aren't the central features in my novel.

Question: In many reviews the book is referred to as sad, melancholic or dark—would you agree with that?

GS: No, I wouldn't, because it's actually a very comic book. Not just because some of the dialogue is very humorous, but because I think its vision of life, its vision of these characters is in the end comic. And that doesn't mean that it's not a serious book. I mean it's highly serious, it deals with some very serious things, but I think it's a novel which is about death in order to be about life, a novel in which death is constantly being interrupted by life. The purpose of the journey is really all to do with death quite clearly, honoring the dead. But it takes them a long time, and they have these diversions and mishaps, fundamentally because life in them is still there and it gets in the way. And all the qualities in their characters don't change simply because it's a special day and they have something special to do. I think it's the way that life is always tripping them up, although their purpose is death, that creates the comedy.

Question: When we were queuing for your reading at the British Council in Cologne, a middle-aged lady was surprised to see so many young people there, expecting your book to be aimed at more mature readers. What kind of reader do you have in mind when you write your books?

GS: I found the story you just told very satisfying, because I don't want to write for any one kind of reader and I don't think of my readers as being a type. They are all sorts of people, young and old, to begin with, so if a middle-aged lady at this reading notices all the young people she's just noticing that there is a range of readers, I find that story really quite pleasing.

Question: Why do you think *Last Orders* is interesting for younger readers?

GS: There is a curious factor in this, your example, that I do have young readers, although most of the characters are certainly older than me in this book, they are a lot older than me. But the comment I would make about that is that I believe very strongly that in a way no character in a book, like no person in life, really belongs to any age. We have an age, and we say: "Oh, I'm fifteen" or "I'm thirty" or "I'm seventy," but we aren't defined by that age, because within us we have all the ages we have been before that, and those things don't go away. So within an old person, there is a young person, and if my characters can show that people belong to all the time that they have lived through, then it might follow that a young person can see in an older character some sort of connection in *Last Orders*. Several of the characters recall quite vividly younger days, so there is something for everyone in my notion of character.

Question: You once said that what sets a good novel apart from other novels is that the reader finds out at the end that he himself has experienced a change. What kind of change did you have in mind?

GS: Well, change may not have been the best word to use. I want to give my readers an experience. I want them to live through something as they read my book so that in a sense they come out, at the end, different from when they went in at the beginning. It's not like a change in the obvious sense. Something has happened which may remain with them and they can repeat it if they read the book again. They undergo something. In that sense there is a change.

Question: But it's nothing specific?

GS: No, it can be different for every reader.

Question: How do you recall your time at university? Was it a good experience? Did it help you in any way to become a writer?

GS: Well, let me explain first of all what I actually did, and I have to go back to the late 1960s, which was a very good time to have been a student. It was a great time to be a student because it was a time when it was good to be young anyway. I went to Cambridge and did a degree at Cambridge, and basically I had a very good time. Then I went on to do a second degree at York University, so I had two kind of periods as a student. Then the second at York was very much a time when I was supposed to be doing some kind of doctoral thesis, but I wasn't. That was when I was really starting properly to write, teaching myself to write. And I used the time at York University to get myself going as a writer. I was pretending to be a student. To answer the other part of your question, my experience at York obviously was valuable for my writing because basically that was what I was doing. Had I not gone to Cambridge, had I not been a student, would I still have become a writer? I think the answer is yes. I don't know how much quicker or slower the process would have been. But I know that my ambition to become a writer began so early, began before real student days and was clearly very strong, and I don't think whether I'd gone to university or not in the end would have mattered. I would have become a writer. And the other thing to be said is that at university I did a lot of reading, and reading is always useful for a writer.

Question: How do you feel about your books being dissected by students and professors of literature? Have you ever received desperate letters by students who just couldn't make out the meaning of this or that detail in your book?

GS: Yes, I'm afraid I have. I'm not suggesting that they're all troublesome letters, but that happens. And the simple fact is, I can't really deal with that, because if I'm trying to answer all the questions students and, indeed, others send to me about my work, I would never do any work. You have to draw a line. I know that theses and dissertations have been written about my work and I know that my books are set texts on various exams. How do I feel about all of that? Well, in one sense it is an honor, because if anyone puts you on an exam course, it suggests that they think that your work has some sort of permanent quality. It's definitely there and it's going to stay. So, that makes me feel good. On the other hand there are two things: I certainly don't write my books so that they're studied. They're to be read. Studying them, like studying any book, is perfectly legitimate, but that is not the purpose of my books. So I very much hope that the students study my work and they don't forget that they can simply read my books as well. The other thing is that I'm a living author, and I can remember most of the books I studied were by dead writers. I resist, but I'm drawn into the process of being a teacher of my own books, I mean that's the danger. So I'll get a request, say, from a university or college: "Will you come along and talk to my students?" And I usually say no, because I don't want to be put in the position where I am the teacher of my books. I'm the writer of my books. My books are there, but actually it is not for me to say how they should be read. It's just for me to offer them for readers.

Question: People speak about a Renaissance of the English novel since the early '80s—do you also read novels by contemporary writers like A. S. Byatt and Julian Barnes?

GS: I read quite a bit. I tend not to read really contemporary writers when I'm in the middle of a novel myself. In fact I tend not to read very much at all when I'm in the middle of a novel. My reading would be preferably classic writing. Or non-fiction. There is a way in which, if you read your contemporaries while you're writing, they can sort of get in the way. So you avoid that. But over the years I've certainly read quite a few of my contemporaries and, of course, I know some of them, some of them are friends.

Question: Why do you think history is such an important topic for contemporary writers?

GS: Well, I can only speak for myself. I would say, first of all, coming back to being a student, I've never been a student of history. I studied literature. I've certainly never been a teacher of history, despite the main character in *Waterland.* That character is not me. I think my interest in history has certainly developed and increased with my writing. First of all, you can't really tell a story without there being a historical dimension, because you tell a story about something that has happened. So the very business of storytelling has a historical quality.

The other thing is that I think one of the marvelous things that the novel can do is to deal with long periods of time. It has the scope for that. You can deal with several generations of characters and you can certainly deal with peoples' lives seen within a historical context, so that you have the personal history of a character and then you have the history of the world through which they have lived. And we're all like that. And I think the older we get, the more we know that we belong to history. We're not just the individual person that we recognize as us, but we are formed, we're made, we belong to this bigger collective thing. We call it history, for want of a better word, we call it history. But we're all part of it.

Question: Your work is often labelled as historiographic metafiction—have you ever heard of that term? Do you know what it means?

GS: No. (laughs) No and no.

Question: Your novels often deal with persons that lead a life full of disappointment and failure—would you agree that we can only give meaning to our postmodern life by turning it into a story?

GS: No. That would be very sad, very sad indeed, if the only meaning we can give our lives is by turning them into stories. I mean life is life, and life finds its own meanings, its own values. And storytelling is simply an aspect of life. I happen to think it's a very important aspect. I happen to think that storytelling is very deep within human nature. It's something that we need, we can't do without it. It certainly doesn't follow from that that the purpose of our lives is to turn ourselves into stories. From time to time, we might be particularly interested in telling our own story, we might feel a particular need to tell our own story. But that isn't the purpose of being in the world generally. And I would say that the urge to tell our own stories occurs particularly in dealing with some sort of crisis, when something very bad or demanding happens to us. It can tend to upset our sense of ourselves and our experience, it can be very disintegrating. Only one of the ways that we have of trying to collect ourselves again is by going through some process of telling a story of what has happened or telling a story of what led to this difficult event. I think we all do that, in different ways, and some more consciously than others. But I mean it's a real instinct within us.

Question: Most of the male characters in your books fail to give a meaning to their lives. You seem to suggest that women haven't got that problem as long as they can give birth to a child and thus give meaning to their existence.

GS: I would make a broader comment. I would say, if this isn't internally circular, that the meaning of life is not to find the meaning of life. I would say it's a mistake to suppose that there is any meaning of life which you can discover and possess, which is somehow going to transform you. If you've found the meaning of life, then surely that can only bring you to the end of life. What would be left to do? In a strange way the marvel of life is that it is perpetually confusing and that it has no single meaning or single purpose, although we often imagine that one is required. So many meanings of life are offered for people to follow or for people to obey, which—you only have to look at history—are clearly insufficient or prejudiced or whatever. And perhaps life is this confusing thing. I think one thing that a novel can do is simply to show that. It can be honest about the fact that life for most of us is actually a confusing process. Most of us don't find any meaning to life, whether we suppose if we shall or not.

Question: Is there any special piece of advice you would give young writers?
GS: Oh dear. People think it's a very strange thing to say, but what I say is you should try to write about what you don't know. People find this strange, because the opposite is much more commonly offered as advice: write about what you know; don't begin to write until you know something. The reason why I say write about what you don't know is that I as a writer place enormous faith on imagination. And imagination, I always think, is a means of getting to what you don't know.

In other words, the whole point of fiction, and it wouldn't be fiction if it didn't do this, is to get away from yourself into experiences of other people, into different worlds, into different lives. In other words, into areas that you don't exactly, let's say, know about, that you can imagine. It's all about imagining what it's like to be somebody else. And that is, after all, one of the most important tasks of life. If we didn't live at least to imagine what other people's lives are like, then we would fail. We would fail as human beings, we would fail as societies. And the novel, among many other things, . . . One of the things the novel can do, is to stimulate that process. And people sometimes criticize the novel, maybe they criticize bad novels, of being an escape. They talk about the escapism of novels as if that is a bad thing. If it is badly written, yes it might be bad. But I think, at the very least, what a novel should do is provide a kind of escape, a liberation from someone's normal self into something else. It is terribly important.

Question: Thank you very much for the interview.
GS: Thank you, all of you!

A Conversation with Graham Swift

Lewis Burke Frumkes / 1998

Originally published in *The Writer* vol. 111. 2 (Feb. 1998): 19–22.
Reprinted by permission of the author.

Lewis Frumkes: British novelist Graham Swift's most recent book, *Last Orders* (Vintage), won the Booker Prize, England's most prestigious literary award, in 1996. He is also the author of *Waterland*, which was made into a film, and *Shuttlecock*. Let me begin by asking him what *Last Orders* is about.
Graham Swift: The main story is the story of a rather peculiar and special journey, a journey which four men undertake in a car to dispose of the ashes of a fifth man, Jack, a butcher from the east end of London. He left this mysterious request that his ashes should be taken and scattered into the sea at a seaside resort about sixty miles from London. These men get together to carry out this wish. The significant thing is that Jack's widow, Amy, decides not to join them, and there is a mystery involved in that.

LF: Which we shouldn't totally reveal. John Barth, in a recent book, wrote about taking a voyage somewhere. There are a number of books dealing with life and death that are philosophically profound, and somehow have to do with water, traveling on the water, to the water. Your most successful book was *Waterland*. What does water mean to you?
GS: I've written *Waterland* and water, or at least the sea, features very much in *Last Orders*. I've also incidentally written a collection of stories called *Learning to Swim*, so there is water again. I have kind of resisted the connection. I do see that, particularly after *Last Orders*, it does play some deep part in our sense of the overall direction of life: Where do we go to, where do we come from? The sea, in particular, I think has always represented the "beyond"; what, if anything, lies beyond life.

LF: What catalyzed you to write about someone's death?

GS: The bigger question: Where did the whole novel come from? It is a question which, to be perfectly honest, I can't answer. I can never really say where novels come from. I'm not the kind of writer that says, "Now I want to write a book about a big theme, like death," for example, and then set about doing it. It evolves in a more mysterious and more fragmentary way. What is going on, really, is that these characters have this very serious and solemn purpose: They want to honor their dead friend. But all the time, life is getting in the way of that. And the life within the characters is tripping them up all the time, and that's where the comedy occurs, it's when life gets in the way of death.

LF: I often ask writers if they work from a well-scripted outline, or whether a novel is character driven. How does it work for you?

GS: It's never well planned. Or, if it's planned, there are lots of gaps and holes in the plan. I think I write a lot by sheer instinct, by groping around in the dark.

LF: And you get into your characters?

GS: Yes, I have always written in the first person. One day I might write in the third person, but I think that I'm happy with the first person, because it does give me that very intimate access into the character. And I like to write at the character's level, from the character's point of view. I get very involved in the characters. I feel extremely close to the characters in this novel, I'm very fond of them.

LF: When did you first start writing, and how did you evolve as a writer?

GS: Well, I think the evolution would have started pretty early on. I was around twelve, thirteen, when I first began to want to be a writer, which is a different thing from discovering that you have any talent to be a writer. I think it came from nothing other than that I read a lot. I'm talking about the 1950s, when, certainly in our home, there was no TV, so reading or listening to the radio was one form of entertainment. I grew up with a sense of the word, and particularly with reading. There was a point at which I became captivated by this magic that writers achieve within the covers of a book, and I suppose I just thought that I would like to do that stuff. But it was a long time after that before I began the process of teaching myself to write. And a long time after that again, before I felt ready to send things off to see if I could get them in print. I went through the process that all writers go through of having them sent back, a long and sometimes lonely struggle. My first novel was published in 1980, but I'd been writing for fifteen years before that. I think it's the typical story.

LF: What writers were you reading when you were that young?
GS: Well, they were certainly not great works of literature. They were the regular sort of kid stuff, boys' adventure stories. I honestly can't remember titles and authors, but reading was important, and I think that first contact with reading is, very often, most important for a potential writer.

LF: You obviously love language. Do you have favorite words, words that crop up more often than other words in your own writing, or words that you think are particularly beautiful, for any reason?
GS: There is one word, which I think is wonderful. It is the word "throb." It is one of those words that simply sounds like what it is. There could be no other word for the thing, as it were. There are a lot of Anglo-Saxon words that have that quality. Even without knowing other languages I am aware of the richness of English. The mixture of influences in the English language is marvelous. And it all comes together with this wonderfully concrete, physical Anglo-Saxon stuff.

LF: Where were you educated?
GS: I come from south London, I went to school in south London, and when I say school, I am talking about the very early part of education. Then I went to Cambridge University and studied English literature. It was a great time to be a student, because this was the late '60s. I was at Cambridge for three years, and then I went on to do a second degree from another university, at York. It was while I was there that I really got down to writing. It was a very valuable time for me. I was a student for six years, and when I stopped being a student, I had the problem of any aspiring writer, what do you do to eat? I've had all kinds of jobs. The one that was my main bread and butter was part-time teaching. But I've worked in a mental hospital, I've been a security guard. All quite useful stuff for a writer, of course. And then the point came, after *Waterland* was published, when I said, "This book seems to be quite successful, I will take the risk and give up any other job, and see if I can live by writing." Happily, I have managed to do that ever since.

LF: Do you write around the clock, in the morning, at night? Do you wait for inspiration?

GS: I believe in whatever it is that we, for convenience sake, call inspiration—that mysterious thing that sometimes happens, not so often, but it does happen. I would say that my writing day has a theory and a practice. The theory is that I start early, as early as six o'clock in the morning. It is a wonderful time of the day when you cannot be interrupted, and if I start that early, by lunch time I can say to myself, "I've done a day's work," and I can then go out to play. But it rarely works like that. And the fact is if my morning work is going well, I don't want to stop. If it's going badly, I want to carry on to put it right. Which means that I end up working a very long day. One discipline I don't have is the discipline of stopping, which is actually very important. I know that sometimes the best thing I can do is get away from the desk and do something completely different. But I'm not very good at doing that. I stick to my post.

LF: Do you work on a computer, or longhand, or a typewriter?
GS: All the original writing, the real composition, I do with pen and ink. I always shall. There is something about the flow of ink, when it flows, which is good. I have a computer, and I certainly recognize the value of computers. They are wonderful for the final stages, for all the later drafts and revisions. But all my real writing is pen and ink. And I think that with a pen, you can make little marks, little messages, for the next page, for what's coming ahead, which actually no computer can do as quickly.

LF: You have won a lot of prizes, but the Booker Prize puts you in very august company. Has that changed your life in any important way? What does it mean to you to have won the Booker Prize?
GS: Well, it certainly hasn't changed my life. I won the prize back in 1996, and I am not aware of being a different person, or indeed being a different writer. In that sense, it has changed nothing. And of course, writers don't write to win prizes, they write for different reasons. That said, it has been a delight to win this prize. I'm thrilled. And of course, it has meant a lot more recognition, a lot more attention, a lot more readers. I would say that I won the Booker Prize at a pretty good time. I've been around for a while, as a person and as a writer. *Waterland* was up for the Booker Prize over ten years ago and was short-listed. A lot of people thought it might win.

LF: Including you?
GS: I had my hopes. But looking back, I'm actually quite glad it didn't win. Because I think then, all those years ago, it might have been too much

success too early. The fact is that *Waterland* has been a very successful book, and it did very well without winning the Booker Prize. But now I've got six, seven books behind me, and I think I'm better able to handle all that is involved in winning a big prize, and more important, to enjoy it.

LF: Do you have writers, either old or contemporary, whom you admire greatly, whom you look to as models for writing styles?

GS: The truth is that everything a writer reads influences him: the great, the good, the bad, and the ugly. And the influences are not always conscious, they are just there; you are not aware of them. I would mention one, a Russian writer called Isaac Babel, who wrote in the '20s and '30s. He is certainly one of those writers, the important influences, not the ones that might actually shape your style and the way that you use words.

LF: You have said you've taught a little bit. What would you advise young writers starting out?

GS: People have occasionally taken issue with this, but my advice would be to write about what you don't know. The standard advice is to write about what you do know. But fiction is about the imagination, and imagination means getting from what you know to what you don't know. The great challenge, the great excitement, the great magic of writing fiction is getting out of yourself, and getting into the lives of other characters; into experiences that are not your own, but sort of become your own as you write. And I think that is done by taking that risk, taking that leap into the unknown. If you write literally only about what you know, you are really writing fact rather than fiction. There have been, of course, wonderful novels that are mainly autobiographical. But I think in the end, your own life, your own experience, provides you with only limited fuel. And the imagination has to do the rest of your work. I think the imagination is a marvelous kind of mental transportation. It can take you to new and exciting places.

Interview with Graham Swift

Lidia Vianu / 2000

From *Desperado Essay-Interviews*, Editura Universității din București, 2006.
Reprinted by permission of the author.

LIDIA VIANU: Among other things, I mean by Desperado a person who mixes literary genres in a unique blend. In *Waterland*, you combine fiction, poetry, history, essay, diary, even teaching, in a Faulknerian bewitching medley. Do you feel this is a feature that brings you together with writers like Julian Barnes, Alasdair Gray, Kazuo Ishiguro, to name only a few disparate examples? Do you do it deliberately or is it as inevitable as breathing, as T. S. Eliot stated about criticism?

GRAHAM SWIFT: I think the mixing of different genres or modes of writing applies only to some of my fiction, especially *Waterland*—though *Shuttlecock* contains a book within a novel and *Ever After* a journal within a novel. I don't think this is either my principal approach to writing or something I have consciously intended or developed. You go where the spirit takes you or do what a particular narrative demands. The book within a book, for example, is a way of setting up a sort of dramatic dialogue between living and dead characters, between past and present, which of course can't literally occur. In *Waterland* the impression of a medley perhaps reflects my ambition at the time of writing. It was my third novel, I felt I could take risks, experiment and stretch myself in ways I hadn't done before. None of this, however, was for its own sake or simply to draw attention to itself, it had to be justified. It was wonderful, for example, to have created a narrative fabric in which it was possible to insert what is almost an essay on the natural history of the eel, but the chapter on the eel has its relevance and purpose within the whole. The recent tendency in my writing has been away from this sort of authorial mixing of styles towards a tone that's governed by my characters. *Last Orders* is also a "mixture," but a mixture of several first-person voices and narratives. The story is pieced together by the characters.

The author, I hope, seems hardly present. I don't group myself with other contemporary writers or feel that I'm part of some collective undertaking. Critics like to make these connections but I think the extent to which writing is a very singular process is often under-estimated. When you write a novel you go away and, for a long time, do something all on your own. Your word "Desperado" intrigues me. It's not how I'd describe myself—though writing can have its share of desperation! On the other hand, "Desperado" perhaps conveys some of the individualism of writing. To write a novel, you need, in a way, to outlaw and uproot yourself. It's a solitary adventure that one day, perhaps, your readers might share.

LV: Stream of consciousness writers like James Joyce and Virginia Woolf meant to smash the narrative and submerge fiction in lyricism. You are also overwhelmingly lyrical, but in a totally different manner. You have returned to the pleasure of the well-told story and enjoy the narrative. Your account of it is meant to baffle and instigate the reader to active rereading. Between lyricism and the narrative, which is dearer to you? Would you like to be called a poet or a novelist, or both? Do you complicate your narration willfully or is it inevitable, again?

GS: The story, the narrative is the most important thing but I'm very happy if my fiction is also felt to have a poetic element. I've written scarcely any poetry in the formal sense. I suppose I'd prefer to write the kind of prose that can become poetry rather that the kind of poetry that might become prose! In any case, I don't think 'poetry' is something that just belongs to verse. My writing may sometimes be "lyrical," though that word, to me, suggests a conscious striving after beauty and rapture. More generally, I'd say that one function of fiction is simply to celebrate what's worth celebrating about life. I hope my fiction does this, even as it may also explore some of the darker areas of life. I believe that there's an innate celebration in any act of creation. I think storytelling, however sophisticated and modern we may get about it, answers a deep need in human nature. There's something primitive and magical about it. If my narratives get complicated, it's not willful. I think life's complicated. Too many people try to simplify it.

LV: Your novels are Mona-Lisa-like narratives, because from every corner a main hero stares at you. You have no minor heroes, they are all minds in progress, brought to the front. Their stories mingle, the novel is a merry-go-round meant to shock the reader into remembrance of things past. Yet history is made present. You choose informal narration and join hands with all readers. This is one face of the Desperado writer: the affectionate narration. If you mean to be close to the reader, how does that go together with your devious amalgamation of incidents in the story? How do you help readers find their way out of the maze of history and feelings brought up to date for each of them?

GS: I tend to prefer first-person narrative—"minds in progress" as you say. This gives you an immediate and intimate access to your character, and in the end implies a certain kind of relationship with the reader too. I want to be 'with' my characters, on their level. I don't want to be superior to them or to pretend to know more than they do. This expresses my basic position as a novelist. I may be an author but I don't think of myself as any kind of "authority." I don't have answers to things—though I have plenty of questions (*Waterland* is full of them) and plenty of doubts. There are a good many people who profess to have answers, to know things, to tell us what is so or what we should do, but this is not what novels are for or why I'm a novelist. An American writer once said we all lead lives of quiet desperation. Perhaps, but I think we all lead lives of quiet confusion. The novel is a form in which you can be true to the confusion of life. I'm not different from my readers and I certainly don't want to have power over them. I'm confused too, I'm in the same boat. I think of the relationship of writer and reader as one of sharing. I want to share confusion—but not directly and, I hope, not unconstructively. So I offer the confusion of my characters who are nonetheless trying to steer some kind of sustainable and hopeful course through their confusion. That course is storytelling. I believe good storytelling can, without denying or misrepresenting the actual confusion of life, redeem it.

LV: You build what a Desperado critic might call delayed plots. Your main device is the constant interruption. It brings suspense and ensures the quality of breathtaking reality. You break chronology (which is an old trick), but you also break the point of view, as the story comes from an "I," a "he," or many such voices (this is much more recent). It happens a lot in *The Sweet-Shop Owner*. Do you value the tricks you use, or are they just means to an end? How much store do you set by innovating the narrative technique?

GS: I don't feel at home with straight, sequential narrative. This partly because I think that moving around in time, having interruptions and delays, is more exciting and has more dramatic potential, but I also think it's more truthful to the way our minds actually deal with time. Memory doesn't work in sequence, it can leap to and fro and there's no predicting what it might suddenly seize on. It doesn't have a chronological plan. Nor does life, otherwise the most recent events would always be the most important. I'd hate to think that any narrative technique I use is merely a trick, and I don't believe in technical innovation for its own sake. Novels shouldn't be novelties. I think I have quite a strong sense of form, but form for me is governed by feeling, by the shaping and timing of emotion. I think there's a connection with music, since music ultimately obeys an irrational, emotional logic. Music is also, famously, a language without words, and, though it may seem odd for a writer to say it, I have a respect for the wordless. The wordless things are often the most important things. I don't think of myself as possessing words, I have to find them, and it's a writer's task to try to find words for things that may be ultimately beyond words or very hard to express clearly. I certainly don't think words (though I love them) are an end in themselves. They're a window to something. So often the best words, words which directly and accurately transmit feeling, are the least noticeable. It means much more to me if a reader says they were moved and gripped by something I've written than if they say they admired my words.

LV: You inherit devices from Henry James (the multiple point of view), Virginia Woolf, William Faulkner, and you do one thing they never dared do: in your novels, your solitary characters abolish the future. You go beyond the stream of consciousness, you upgrade it, so to say. Do you feel related to old techniques? How would you define your own identity, whether Desperado or not?
GS: I think my answer to the previous question really covers this. I wouldn't want to define or categorize myself in literary terms. This is for critics to do. If there's anything "new" in my work then it's because my subject-matter has demanded it, not because I seek "newness." Originality is a real virtue but I think it resides in the unique spirit and vision that can belong to an individual author, not simply in the devising of new things. While I'm sure I belong to my time (in ways that I may not always be aware of) I have a healthy respect for past writers and their "old techniques." It's the content that matters, the techniques are secondary. The content—human nature—doesn't change that much. I want to write about the things we have in common and matter most and perennially to us, the core of human experience. New clothes don't alter the flesh and blood underneath.

LV: *Out of This World* and *Shuttlecock* are intensely personal experiences, related with an eye open to irony. How do you make lyricism and irony coexist? Would you agree that this is a typical feature of your generation, the Desperado writers?

GS: Lyricism and irony can coexist, and need to—imagine looking at the world entirely without one or the other. I'm a great believer in 'this *and* that,' in complexity, even paradox. Confusion again! The title of one of my novels— *Waterland*—is itself an ambiguity, a "both" not an "either/or." I'm fascinated by borderline conditions, or rather by the difficulty of drawing a distinct line between some fundamental human concerns—between past and present, say, or history and story. There's an even more impossible line, which I think all writers of fiction sooner or later come to reflect on—the line between what we agree to call the real world and a world that exists but mainly in our heads, the world of imagination, memory and invention. In short, the line between fact and fiction. I think we're all hybrid, ambiguous creatures inhabiting both worlds and we can be lyrical about each. As soon as we're aware of how imprecise the border is between the two, irony steps in.

LV: One central theme of your novels is the connection, the relationship of parents-children. It has ups and downs, the generation gap is painfully present, but overcome. Parenthood is a highly awkward position. Are you ever autobiographical in what you write? Are your novels so lyrical because of the burden of their author's sensibility?

GS: I agree. Parent-child and cross-generational relationships are every-where in my work. I don't think I'm peculiar in this: being someone's son or daughter or being someone's father or mother are fundamental human experiences and have always been written about. People say I write intensely and intimately about the parent-child relationship, but I don't have children myself. This is a good example of how I'm not an "autobiographical" writer. In general, I'm against the autobiographical approach to fiction—turning your own direct experiences into the stuff of fiction. I don't base my charac-ters on people I know, or on myself. Good things have been written in this way but I think it's a sort of anti-fiction, since it's really fact in disguise. The biggest challenge and reward in fiction—it's what fiction's *for*—is to enter experience *other* than your own, yet to identify with it—to try to know what it's like to be someone else. In any case, fiction should create and discover. It can't do this if its only source is the personal. Of course, at the deepest level, every novelist's work must be about himself or herself—where else does it come from?—but there's no reason why your direct personal experiences should be interesting to anyone else and they can only provide limited mate-rial. Sooner or later you have to *imagine*. I believe it's the author's imagining (as opposed to mere recounting) that sets alight the reader's imagination and provides the special thrill of fiction: that something that we know is made up can yet become alive and authentic, can be felt as real and true, as if it's happening to us.

Returning to parent-child relationships, my own childhood was quite happy and secure, and my relations with my parents good. So the autobiographical explanation wouldn't account for the many unhappy or vexed family situations in my work—and, incidentally, writers are generally supposed to emerge from *unhappy* childhoods! Another point I'd make about relationships across the generations is that they are simply something the novel has scope for. The novel can deal, preeminently, with long periods of time, with historical perspective, with whole lives and the changes they undergo, and this can be extended to dealing with more than one generation, indeed several. As a matter of literary opportunity as well as of broad philosophy, it would be a shame not to explore this possibility.

LV: Your fiction invites quotation. Memorable sentences could be short, haiku-like poems. The situations you build are symbolic and deeply tender, touching. You build lives more than real plots. The plot of your novels is simple, its complications and life cargo are endless. Lyrical disorder seems to be your halo. Breaking the order of sensibility is a Desperado feature (the stream of consciousness broke conventions, but Desperadoes break the broken soul). What is the real way you want your readers to follow when they read you?
GS: I like the idea of "building lives" and I like the expression "life cargo." My immediate narrative and plot may not require that the full history of a character, who may be in their middle or late years, is known. But my instinct would be to delve, at least a little, into the earlier life of that character, even where it doesn't seem relevant—it may become relevant. I think characterization itself partly depends on having a sense of the character's existence before they entered, as it were, the immediate story—just as in life we get a better understanding of and sympathy for someone, if we learn what they were like before we met them. A sense of what an adult was like as a child, that they *were* indeed once a child, can open a door into them. I have often tended to write about characters older than myself (though I don't get any younger!): I think I respect the freight, the weight of experience. In any case, I have a strong faith that nobody is ever only what they are at any one time. We contain our former selves, even when we may think we have shed them. So inside the old man is still the youth and the child. All the persisting layers

of accumulated experience make up the person, the unique life. It's never just what you see. I think the novel is wonderfully equipped to illuminate this. I'm touched if any of my sentences are memorable enough for quotation and if some of my situations have a symbolic power. I hope this has something to do with my desire to write about that core of experience common to us all. I hope I touch the universal, but I learn more and more that the key to the universal is in the particular and the local. Novels aren't statements, they're actual, particular experiences—experiences we can add to other experiences in our lives. When we come to the end of a good novel we have the feeling of having lived through something. That's what I'd like my readers to have, an experience.

LV: *Ever After* is a novel on lost love, lost history, lost love of life, yet somehow intense presence of all these. The novel, like all the others, is an endless goodbye. You use, among other tricks (such as mingling history and contemporaneity), intertextuality. You quote a diary that records not only the previous century, but actually an experience of the whole history of mankind. You have a desire for globality. It is all in the memory-land of your characters' stories. Do you write with your mind (understanding of everything you know) or with your soul (lyrical perception of the world)?
GS: I hope I write with my soul first and my mind (remembering what I've said about knowledge and confusion) second. But I think you have to write with both—heart and head. This question highlights *Ever After* and its sense of loss, its valedictory quality, but I think these things may be an inherent part of all storytelling. We tell a story because something *has* happened. We are made to contemplate the past—and what's passed. Stories give us hindsight but also lead us to a sense of transience, mortality. This needn't be sad or dispiriting, however, since it's in the very nature and energy of stories to provide a defense against time, a glow against dark. Stories are on the side of life, they go with life—even when they're about death. *Ever After* is partly a love story which reverses the familiar pattern. It starts with an unhappy ending and ends with a happy beginning. My latest novel, *Last Orders*, is in certain obvious ways about death, but it's about death in order to be about life. It's often—literally and comically—about life getting in the way of death. That, I think, is only how it should be.

Graham Swift

Robert Birnbaum / 2003

From *Identity Theory, a literary website, sort of*. © Robert Birnbaum/Duende Publishing 2018. Reprinted by permission of the author.

Graham Swift was born in London, attended Cambridge University and York University and is the author of seven novels, *The Sweet-Shop Owner, Shuttlecock, Waterland, Out of This World, Ever After, Last Orders* (which was awarded the Booker Prize in 1996), *The Light Of Day* and a short story collection, *Learning to Swim*. His writing has won numerous awards and has been translated into twenty-five languages. Graham Swift is a Fellow of the Royal Society of Literature and lives in London with his wife and eventually will begin working on his next novel.

The Light of Day is a story of one day in the life of George Webb, a middle-aged, divorced, former police detective who is now a private investigator. In this day we learn of George's childhood, his marriage, his relationship with his daughter, his police career and his love affair with a convicted and imprisoned murderess. Anthony Quinn in the *New York Times* opines, "He [Swift] has become a master of word paring and phrase-clipping and scene-whittling and the austerity of style feels like a perfect fit with the voice of his laconic detective."

Robert Birnbaum: I looked over your press portfolio and looked at the review in *Publisher's Weekly*—which is, of course, quite favorable.
Graham Swift: I've never seen it.

RB: Well, here it is, the forecast, "It's been nearly seven years since the publication of *Last Orders*, and an expectant readership may well justify Knopf's seventy-five thousand first printing. Lovely cover art won't hurt."
GS: (both laugh)

RB: Here's the review: "George Webb, a divorced ex-cop and the narrator of this fine novel, works as a private investigator in London (emphasized, because the novel takes place in Wimbledon). Specializing in matrimonial work, blah, blah, blah. Nash, whose client knows the truth of the affair already, . . . She is just looking for a sign that her husband can love her again."
GS: I am starting to lose it already.

RB: "Webb's movements on a particular day in November furnish the opportunity to learn about his childhood." I could go on. I look at this and I think that is difficult to write short, to summarize a novel in three hundred words.
GS: Well, as I say I haven't read that before. But I have read similar pieces where the facts and the way the plot works, they got that wrong. And there is not really an excuse for it, is there?

RB: No. But what I was fascinated by was the forecast. This is a reality of the world that you inhabit and toil in. Has it taken seven years to write this novel?
GS: On paper as it were it will seem it will be seven years since the original publication of *Last Orders*. But the reality is that, well, firstly, my time was taken up by my last book, running around for it. Not a complaint—it was a success. I did a lot of stuff. It was effectively two years. I don't mean two solid years, two years in which my time was being interrupted so I couldn't get back.

RB: Then you had that damn award [The Booker Prize].
GS: Exactly. So before I could even sit down and pursue the next novel, find the subject for it, a couple of years had gone by. And then at the other end, of course, there is no reason that the public should be aware of this—I delivered *The Light of Day* over a year ago. So a year has already gone by since the finishing of that book. The real gap is four years or so, which is still a long time, but it's about the time that it takes for me.

RB: Why do you think it's a long time?
GS: I don't actually think it's a long time. But I know that several people would.

RB: Your publisher and your agent?
GS: No, not them. But there are people who think of writers as, every year a new book. And there are such writers, of course. But I am not one of them.

RB: Do you feel any pressure from that?
GS: No I don't. I don't set out to see how many books I am going to write. That's not the object of the exercise. It takes as long as it takes. Another

thing that happens is you don't get it right the first time. You set out and stop and say, "No, that's not right. I'll go back to the beginning." That uses up time. But it's good time. That can be tough, but I think that one of the ways I have, dare I say it, matured as a writer is in the process of saying to myself, "No that is not good enough." And rejecting my own work and in some cases starting again.

RB: Any thoughts on how many people in the world look at their lives this way?
GS: [pause] I would guess not many.

RB: I ask because given that I expect there is a shortfall in understanding who lives their lives in this way.
GS: That may be true too. I am talking to you on how it is. I don't expect that sort of understanding. In the end I produce a novel and it is there for the public. It is there for the reader and it's not part of the package that they should know how it was for me as I wrote it . . .

RB: But they want to.
GS: I know they are interested.

RB: They want to know your shoe size.
GS: But it's not necessary. Again, it's not what it's really all about.

RB: In the "Writers on Writing" series that the *New York Times* does, Ann Beattie had voiced the opinion to the effect that writers are overexposed. These days they are tripping all over each other on book tours. Whatever the conclusions to be drawn from that, something that one might consider is it the audience's hunger for contact with writers and therefore make extraneous information more common or the desire of the writer to get out of that lonely room and meet other sentient beings?
GS: Well, all this has happened in my writing life. When I began writing, which is now some time ago—when I say began, this is long before I was ever published—my sense of the writer then, the world's sense of the writer then going back a few decades, was essentially of this person you never saw. They might have a photo on the back of the jacket of the book, but they sat somewhere and they wrote and they delivered their books to a publisher who published their book and meanwhile the writer remained where they were and possibly carried on with another book. All that has changed dramatically. And it's taken some adjusting.

RB: [laughs]

GS: It really has. Because I am not the natural, out-on-the-road kind of writer. That's not really me. But such is the real world of books now that you have to do some of that. I guess I have adjusted to doing it. If I hadn't, I wouldn't be sitting here with you now. But I would agree with Anne Beattie that this has been quite a detrimental process in some ways. However it might have helped the public, the readers feel that authors are these invisible people, they are real human beings that they can occasionally see and meet, I think it has cut down, quite seriously sometimes, on the time and concentration of the writer at his or her work.

RB: You are expected to participate in these subsidiary activities as part of your responsibility as a writer. It seems that support systems have improved. Aggressive agents, who sometimes take the places of what editors used to do . . .

GS: Yeah.

RB: Hot shot PR firms, smart publishers . . .

GS: Well, I have an agent. I certainly wouldn't call him aggressive.

RB: He is not Andrew Wylie?

GS: No, I can safely say that. He may be aggressive with publishers, but I don't see that. My agent is such a very good friend. He has been my agent for many years. I think what you just said is partly true though the role of the editor . . . the publisher's editor has been eroded to the extent that sometimes it is the agent who is the real confidante of the author, the close companion of the author. That is something else that has happened in my writing life and the other thing, damn it, is that publishing itself has changed. When I started out back home there was a long list of publishing houses and imprints. The names are still there, but they have been coalesced into these big conglomerates.

RB: Coalesced. (laughs)

GS: The actual choice of publishers now is more limited. And they are constantly changing anyway.

RB: That is true in England also?

GS: Oh yes.

RB: Equally as in the US?

GS: That's my suspicion. The things become international anyway. There is a Random House here, there is a Random House UK. I think the one thing that you can say now is that a consistent factor in all this, the factor of which you could say in five years' time, they are still going to be basically the same, is the author. In five years' time, God willing, I shall still be me. I hope still producing what I produce. I can promise that so far I can. No publisher can make the promise they will still be the same in five years' time. No way. Even in a year's time.

RB: What difference does it make if it's the editor or the agent who is giving intelligent advice from the writer's point of view but from the publishing houses it must make a difference that editors have changed their roles and attitudes and allegiances?

GS: I think so. The unfortunate shift is that the marketing departments for the publishing house have become more important than the editorial ones. With some good exceptions. But the whole business is marketing led now in way that it wasn't twenty or thirty years ago.

RB: It wouldn't be fair to single out publishers for this development. All businesses seem to be marketing driven.

GS: But you can still say, nonetheless, about publishing that it has this cultural dimension. Of course, it's commerce. Of course you want to sell books. That is true. It's legitimate but there is a cultural dimension to it. So why are people in it? Surely they have to recognize that. If it's just about commerce then sell something else.

RB: [laughs] Yeah, I remember Molly Ivins telling that if you think people are stupid then go into advertising. I was reading something that quoted Samuel Johnson on a dinner party he had attended, "A lot of talk and not much conversation." From that observation I was thinking about this character George Webb who spends his time in this novel thinking about the past. Not all of it particularly insightful or profound.

GS: Yes, go on.

RB: Then it struck me that we don't really think brilliant and original thoughts very much. Most of our thoughts are humdrum and quite ordinary.

GS: That's certainly an area that I am at home in. I am the kind of writer—it should be pretty obvious—who certainly starts with the ordinary world. The world around the corner, the familiar world. And if there is going to be anything extraordinary, I will find it in that. Of course, there is something extraordinary. There are many extraordinary things. What you just said about how many things are said in a day that are really significant is another question. How many things are thought which are significant but never get said?

In a way, a more tantalizing question. Such is my faith in human nature that I think . . .

RB: Go easy . . .

GS: I'll be cautious. But the saying things and then articulacy you need to say them. I think we often have the thoughts and the feelings and those thoughts and feelings go unsaid because the words don't immediately come out. In my new novel and in *Last Orders*, I was in part trying to give a voice—if I can put it like that, to people's inner thoughts and perceptions. You have to be very careful with this because the language that I, the author, use must not condescend to the character must not betray where that character was coming from. But I was trying to do that thing of saying, "Well this man or woman might never have actually said that in so many words but they could well have had the thought, the perception that goes with those words." And George, the central character in *The Light of Day*, is in that situation. That is to say, he would have called himself a not very well-educated man. Educated but not very well educated. He says often, "Words were not my thing." He's a policeman and a detective and thought of himself as a man of action, if anything. Something has happened to him now, which has transformed his life. And transformed his whole perception of the world. And in a way, his sense of words and language. And he is seeing the world anew in this novel and needing to find ways of articulating what he is seeing.

RB: There were two instances in the book that resonated for me. One, when he learns something about his daughter that he hadn't known before. There is a very flat response, but it's not like he hasn't heard what she has told him. You didn't overplay that scene . . .

GS: Let's focus on that for a moment. The situation is he has had a terrible relationship with his daughter. He's is now a man in his middle years. His daughter is approaching thirty. When she was young, a teenager, they were at war. It seemed she hated him and he couldn't do anything about it. And then there is this point later on in life when she finally says to him, "Look, Dad, I'm a lesbian."

RB: She doesn't actually say that.

GS: She doesn't put it in that way. He asks, "Is there anyone in your life?" And she says, "As a matter of fact there is. She is called Claire." She is admitting something that she has never admitted before. He never realized. But in a flash he knows there was all that trouble in the past. In a flash he feels guilty because he didn't know and because if he had he could have understood her. But he understands her right now. And then the next thought that flashes through his head is, "What do I say?" And he's thinking, "Actually, it's okay that she said this. It's not a problem. But if I just say, 'That's all right,' she's going to think that, 'My God, for years I've kept this a secret and I have confessed to him and he's just saying it's okay.'" So he thinks, "Should I make a big deal about it? Should I behave like a father might behave in this situation and sort of sound off about it all?" But in the end he just does the right thing. A word of love that gets said. And suddenly this relationship is completely mended.

RB: I have no idea what his wife's problem was with him? Except she is a lapsed Catholic.

GS: Well, there is an element of that. The breakup occurs when his career as a policeman is finished and he gets kicked out of the police for improper police behavior and part of her reaction is really a judgement. She is a pretty judgmental woman. There are plenty of other things leading up to the breakup, but this is the last straw for him.

RB: I saw her as a terminally dissatisfied person, but I don't know what her beef, as we say in America, was with him.

GS: Ah, she is a teacher, so one factor is perhaps that it doesn't look good for her purposes that she is married to this guy that has been kicked out of his job in this way. But I think there are a whole number of contributing factors. It's ironic that she is a teacher because the central female character in the novel is also a teacher, although she is no longer a teacher in the sense that she is in prison. But she carries on teaching in one sense because part of the relationship between her and George, her visitor in prison, is a sort of teacher-student relationship. It's not the primary relationship, but it does work like that.

RB: This may be oblique, but trust me, this may get somewhere. The size and shape of the book is interesting to me. If it were a usual book size it would have been a thinner book. As it stands now it is a 320-page book, but it seems to take less time to read than one would expect from a book of such length. Was the book (5" x 7") designed to make it look larger—perhaps to slow the reader down?

GS: Well, what you said is interesting, because another way in which I hope I have progressed as a writer is in the direction of economy and concision in the direction of saying quite a lot in a few words and even then saying it with quite simple words. This is not a wordy book, if I can put it like that. I hope if I ever was a wordy writer that I have become a less wordy writer. And my sense of writing, more and more—this is something I have said before— is that what you are dealing with really is what lies beyond the word. The words themselves are not the be all and end all of writing. They are only there to give something, to transmit something. And that's why often the best words are the least noticeable words, because they are transparent. The feeling comes through. So, in that sense my novels have reduced, fewer words, simpler words. But I hope what lies beyond is always expanding, if I can put it like that.

RB: Here's what I am getting to. I believe Edgar Allan Poe suggested a novella was a story that one would sit down after dinner and be compelled to finish the reading in one sitting. Did you have any thoughts about whether this story would be best digested in one sitting—especially since this all takes place in one day of George's life?

GS: If someone sat down and started it and didn't get up again until they finished that's fine by me. There is no obligation to read the book in that way.

RB: [laughs]

GS: But if they did that that's fine. I guess I like to feel that I can have it both ways. That I have written the kind of book which might affect the reader like that, which would be read in one sitting and that would be fine. But at the same time a book that can be slowly digested and certainly a book, whether it was read the first time at a single sitting or not could be reread with increasing satisfaction. Or reward or whatever.

RB: I, as I would suppose of other readers, would aspire to reread books but one of the inhibitors is that there are so many new books. I just read Robert Stone's new novel twice because I felt distracted the first reading. Which got me to thinking about how much I got out of the books I have read the one time.

GS: It's tricky, isn't it? The very notion of reading a book at one sitting and reading a book quickly can be misconstrued. It's like saying it won't take you very long. It won't take up a lot of your time. It will be an undemanding thing. That's hardly what a serious novelist wants. You want to make demands. You want something, which is full of real nourishment. But it is very hard in these days to reread. I think the book culture is for the quick thing. For the one-off thing. So there is no modern contemporary equivalent of the classic book, which is there on the shelf constantly to be reread.

RB: Actually, I have picked out two. I try to reread one of two García Márquez's novels every year, either *One Hundred Years of Solitude* or *Love in Time of Cholera*. It's an arbitrary choice but not less rewarding because of that. What will happen to libraries?

GS: Libraries have gone into a sad state of decay in my country. It's funny, I seem to be deploring all these sad changes but again when I started writing, libraries were good places to be. Pretty well supported by public funds, which they no longer are. Libraries were even places where there was a market for new publications. A serious novelist would expect to have so many copies in libraries and now for obvious reasons that's all changed. The whole communication of books has changed.

RB: There is a persistent, gnawing kind of anxiety that is expressed by books such as Ray Bradbury's *Fahrenheit 451* that we will come to a place and time where there will be no books. But yet there are always signs of hope and you being the optimist about humanity . . .

GS: Well, I am an optimist in many ways and even an optimist about the book. There is now the resurrection of the book. People are often saying the book is finished. Other things will take its place. Actually, look around, the book is still very much there. There are bookstores, still. There are readers. There are people who want this experience that only sitting with a book can give. It's the experience I write for. It's a wonderful, personal, private kind of chemistry which occurs between you and the pages of the book, and it's a very free thing because as we all know every reader reads the book in their own way. They have an experience, which is defined for them. And nothing else really gives that. It's why—as much as I love going to the cinema—I always think that the movies, the screen is smaller than the page because what you get on the screen it may be marvelous but the screen is saying, "This is it." Everyone sitting out there is going to see this and see the same thing. Seeing whatever actor it is playing the character and so on. How different that is when you read a book. I actually, when I am writing I don't have a very strong visual impression of my characters. If you say what's George like in the *Light of Day*? I don't think I could answer that. And that's partly because I want to leave . . .

RB: Sarah wears black cashmere.
GS: Yeah, but that's clothing. She doesn't wear that in prison either. But it's up to the reader to imagine how the character looks.

RB: Well, the end of the literature and the end of civilization and the end of this and that are certainly preoccupations of . . . but I can't help but thinking that the literary universe is of a fixed size. It doesn't get smaller and it doesn't expand . . . and the anxiety that comes about its existence is about it competing with everything else that is getting larger. Growth is a sign of success; thus we want the literary culture to grow as a validation of its importance.
GS: Literary culture is pretty damn old. It has grown. It is what it is and has reached its maturity and is maintaining its maturity and doesn't need to do something to carry on being what it is.

RB: Perhaps it is the anxiety of the marketing departments?
GS: It may well be.

RB: I asked about the notion of reading at one sitting is that his novel takes place in one day but is a meditation on George Webb's life. At that point the idea of one day became meaningless. I found the story to be very full of time.
GS: It is. Yes, it does certainly follow the course of a single day. I do that quite in detail and quite intimately. Almost hour by hour. But that single day, that present day is a hinge on which so much else I hung. Rather typically, I would say, for my kind of narrative. I constantly move around in times— what I naturally do. It's what we naturally do. On any given day, any present day. How many memories will we have in the course of that day? How many other things in our life will, mentally at least, even if we are not entirely conscious of it feature for us on any given day, our whole life is there, on any given day. That's the way it works.

RB: Did you feel required to read detective novels?
GS: No, no . . .

RB: Is it an arbitrary matter that he is a detective?
GS: Well, it's not entirely arbitrary. George was there before he was anything else. He is a human being before he is anything else. The evolution of his

character involved him being other things than being a detective. I won't say what he was but there were earlier stages where George is not a detective. And then a moment came somehow that I knew that he had to be a detective. And that moment was not a moment when I said to myself, "Oh now I am going to write a detective story. Or now I am going to do that sort of thing which is done many times." Nor did I say to myself I want to play around with the genre of the detective story or the murder mystery. Why the hell should I do that? So, it's a novel. It's a serious grown up novel, which has a detective as its main character.

RB: One of the trade publications in their two hundred-word capsule review suggested that the title was a bow to the noirish aspects of the novels of the '30s and '40s.
GS: I wish someone could tell me. Maybe you can. What does 'noir' mean, let alone 'noirish'? What does 'noir' mean?

RB: [laughs]
GS: I am afraid it really doesn't mean anything. I know it's French for 'black.' But when people say 'noir' that is not exactly what they mean. It's a label word and it's bandied about and God's truth I don't know what it means.

RB: Well as long as we are talking about a word that is normally affiliated with cinema, I don't share your feeling about the limitations of film. There is lots implicit and loaded into films. I can think of so many scenes that are just physical gestures by an actor that I think require some interpretation.
GS: I am a bit biased, and I half agree with you. One thing that often happens in cinema when it works is this thing of the little, the minimal thing giving a lot, particularly close-ups. A shot of a character's eyes. All you need sometimes is to see the close up of the eyes of the character or the face of the character, not doing much at all. Given the right context you fill it in, the audience fills in what is going on behind the eyes, as it were. So that's the sort of parallel reverse of something you get with the novel. But I still stick with the novel in the end.

RB: [laugh] I'm glad you said you were biased. Would you be troubled if I read something that I didn't understand?
GS: Go ahead. Maybe I won't understand it either.

RB: "No matter what we do no matter how bad. If we are found to be corrupt. Even if we do the worst thing ever. Even if we do what we never thought was in us to do and kill another person. Even if that other person was once the person for whom we are holding out a net." I just couldn't get my mind around that.

GS: Ah well. It comes from something before in a chapter. I can't really say any more than that. It's the end of a chapter and the effect of those words depends on things that have come before.

RB: Tricky. Challenging.

GS: [both laugh]

RB: That does speak to the quality of one's first reading. How do you know when your story is finished?

GS: By some sort of gut instinct, basically. I guess you could say a book is never finished. You could always fiddle around with it until doomsday. Little tiny touches. You sort of know instinctively that it's now done and it's rarely from a moment of, "Aha, today I finished it." It's not like that, but it dawns on you that it's that.

RB: In *The Light of Day* were you starting with one present day as the container for the story?

GS: No I didn't. I can't remember at what point that decision came but it was a very positive point and a very constructive point. Realizing that there could be this single day that was the hinge for lots of other things. And this after all is something I have done before because *Last Orders* had a similar structure. There is a single present day and it is a special day involving a journey in that novel. And that too acts as a sort of focus for a lot of other stuff and a lot of going back in time.

RB: I was tempted to say that would seem to make the task of finishing the story easier.

GS: It starts in morning with George's arrival at his office just like any ordinary day although this isn't quite an ordinary day. And it finishes technically with him returning to his office and a passage of hours in between. But a passage of a whole lot of other stuff too.

RB: And so you finish the first draft and then what happens?

GS: First, I don't think there is anything as distinct as a draft. That's to say the whole thing from start to finish, even in a rudimentary form but complete nonetheless. I think my drafts are more messy and chaotic things where I might have written some stuff which will be pretty much like the final thing but a lot won't be anything close to the final thing, which I have to discard and rewrite. I would say I probably wrote two and even three times as much as what you got in the finished book, to get to what you have in the finished book. But not necessarily in the form of complete recognizable drafts.

RB: At what point does someone else see it?

GS: Very, very late. Almost the point at which I think I have got it, I've finished, is the point at which I can contemplate showing it to someone else. And that someone else will be my wife first and then one or two people in the trade as it were. I guess those things go together. For me at least, it's a strange paradox, I can spend this time with this something that I am the only person who knows about it but with the object of lots of people knowing about it, in the end. And there has to be a moment where you move from one state to the other.

RB: I am aware that you have friends that are writers. And I imagine you associate with them and such.

GS: Yup, I now know and number among my friends quite a few writers. This is another irony or paradox because certainly there was a time when I wrote without knowing a single other writer and indeed I did that for many years. So there I was, out in the cold, as it were and then gradually I did meet other writers and became good friends with some of them. I think when I get together with them they would say the same thing, I am sure, writing itself is probably the last topic to come up. We respect what each one of does enough to not say, "What are you working on now? How's it going?" that sort of thing. You can probably get the signals anyway, but we talk about anything else but.

RB: What happens if a friend writes a book you just can't abide?

GS: I think I would have the courage to say that. I never had to say that so bluntly. I might say, "I couldn't get on with this one like I got on with the last one." Or something like that. Again that works reciprocally. It would be surprising if someone read several of your books and felt equally about each one of them. Not just a friend but any reader. Different books please different people.

RB: Someone quoted me Gertrude Stein's idea that artists should never be criticized. I would think taking bad reviews and less than glowing commentaries must be hard.

GS: Well, we are all human; we would all prefer to have nice things said about us than not so nice things. I care less and less what the critics and reviewers say. Partly because I have gotten used to that process. I have gotten used to the process, which is a pretty brief one. You publish a book and then for a little while it will be in the papers and people will say things about it but it is a little while—a few weeks. And that's behind you and the book is out there in the real world as it were, and it will find readers and that's what matters. So it's a transient experience anyway. I know what I am doing. I know the worth of what I am doing. If people don't get it, well, too bad. [chuckles]

RB: Well, there are reviewers and there are critics like Michael Dirda and Jonathan Yardley and Gail Caldwell and James Wood who take a broader more contextual view. Do you pay attention to those writers?
GS: I am not terribly up on what comments I have had apart from things I knew about before I came here. I read some of it, I don't make it a job to read everything that is said.

RB: I'm distinguishing reviewers from critics and get your sense of whether they perform a service and whether the criticism is well argued and thought out and knowledgeable?
GS: That is or should or could be a useful distinction—reviewing and criticism. There is a lot of reviewing and you could say there is not a lot of real criticism. A lot of reviewers aren't really critics in the sense that that is their professional activity. They're people doing that job because they got picked to do it that week, that sort of thing. The consistent sort of regular critic is not actually a very common thing these days. Perhaps there should be more of that. But then even if you have a regular critic, the danger is they might occupy a position and get very important about it at the expense of certain intellectual freedoms. It's not a perfect world.

RB: It would seem that more book coverage is better.
GS: Well, it often said that there is no such thing as bad publicity. I wonder. People who say that are often publicists. [both laugh]

RB: Yeah, there are there are these celebrities who do awful things and continue in the limelight. In any case, what is next for you?
GS: When I am through with the current touring—I'm in North America now and there are going to be a number of translations of *The Light of Day,*

starting this fall. I am going to have to do more of this at home or in Europe. But when I am on the other side of that it will be back to the novel writing. I hope. There is something—I was going to say fermenting, but that might be too strong a word, but there is something getting on up there at the moment. So when I can, I'll sit down and put it to the test.

RB: I get the sense that you approach working on a book from start to finish. That is to say, that you could be working on it now on planes and trains or wherever.

GS: In a sense there is no reason, but if you were me I think you'd know . . . I'm certainly not that kind of writer. I can't do more than one thing at one time. I'm afraid that while I'm traveling like this I'm not being very creative. [chuckles]

RB: Do you listen to music when you write?

GS: Not when I write. But I do certainly listen to music and I think music informs my writing. I don't mean any particular music. I just think I have a musical feeling for things even though my business is words and narrative. A lot of the things that occur in music also occur and work in storytelling. Things like rhythm, and timing, and pacing, and so on. And I am a very emotional writer. Music is obviously an emotional language. When I say I am an emotional writer I don't mean that I am constantly tearing my hair out sitting in my room, although I can get like that. I am guided by emotions. My sense of the shape of what I am doing is guided by emotion. It is not an intellectual presence. It has very much to do with feeling and in the end I want to write things that people feel and if someone says to me, "I was moved by what you did, I was gripped, I was compelled by what you did." That means much more than someone saying, "Oh, I did like that description on page thirty-seven." Emotion is central.

RB: Good.

GS: Thank you.

Graham Swift and the Sense of History: An Interview

Juan Gabriel Vásquez / 2003

From *Cuadernos Hispanoamericanos* (CHA) 2003, pp. 99–110. © Juan Gabriel Vásquez, 2003. Translated from the Spanish by Paul B. Nelson.

In June of 2000, two years after having read *Waterland*, I traveled to London to talk with Graham Swift. "Do you like Indian food?" he had written me. "If you do, I suggest we meet at the Bombay Brasserie," a restaurant with a colonial atmosphere that looks as if it were taken from certain pages of Forster. It's located a little to the west of downtown London, on Courtfield Road, an area I was surprised to find, on the shelves of an old bookshop, a copy of the first edition of *Waterland*. When it was published in 1983, the novel confirmed Swift's reputation. It's the story—in lowercase—of a History teacher—in uppercase—who loses his job because his material is no longer considered essential. His personal crisis is resolved through the reconstruction of his and his family's past, a line of brewers who settled in the English Fens several generations ago and who, like the other inhabitants of the area, were used to fighting against the water that invades their lands. Swift, who was born in 1949 on the outskirts of a London devastated by the recent war, has chosen the times before his time as the material for almost all his narratives. His latest novel is *Last Orders* (awarded the Booker Prize). It deals with a deceptively simple plot: a man has died (in Bermondsey, south of London: very close to the place Swift was born) and entrusted his friends to take his remains to the ocean (at Margate, the place Eliot wrote a large part of *The Waste Land*). That's all that happens. But to say that is all that happens while describing, for example, *As I Lay Dying*, would also be, and for similar reasons, a frivolity.

Vásquez: I'd like to begin by talking about a form of the personal story that seems to interest you a lot: the father figure. The father rules the destinies of the characters in *Out of This World*, and in some stories in *Learning to Swim*, and, of course, he is found at the center of *Last Orders*. Your father was a civil servant for the State and was also a naval pilot during World War II. How did he react to your decision to become a writer?

Swift: I don't believe my father understood exactly what writing novels was about. However, unlike what often usually happens, he didn't discourage me. I believe what worried him, above all, was how I was going to live, how I would make a living. I don't come from a family with a literary background, but rather from a humble family, without the habit of reading. We were, to put it in terms of the social hierarchy, from the lower middle class. My father's great lesson was his tolerance: Not understanding something didn't push him to segregate it or to despise it. He was interested in getting the information, and then he would broadcast a concept. One compares oneself to other people, for whom the profession is determined by the moment in which they begin to work in it, and he notices an essential difference. For the beginning writer, the reality of the profession starts only from the moment he can show a review and say: "My work appears here, and my story has been published on this page." Before that, at least for the others (including one's family members), there is nothing. My father wanted security for me, but not if it impeded my wishes. His world was a world of uncertainty, where the war was a source of immense difficulties. He thought about that and then he thought about my world, the world I was born into; and, while some fathers would have opted for a profession that prevented the uncertainties of the war years for their children, he knew how to respect my imagination and my calling. He didn't impose his fears on me; he didn't try to impose on me the certainties and comforts that he never had.

Vásquez: How did you use your father's memories? Did you (two) often talk about the war?

Swift: In reality, not as much as I would have liked. My father spoke little about the war and I rarely asked him. When I did, I felt like I was intruding on someone else's territory and that he would talk when he was ready for it. So I let him come to me to tell me things when he saw fit, and, in the end, that happened less than either of us perhaps wanted. Of course I have often written about the war, but that has very little connection to my father's experience. I'm not an autobiographical writer. It's evident that life itself, in a very essential way, always appears in one's writings, but I don't believe literature tries to tell experience itself. My childhood, for example, was very normal, and often happy, though never idyllic. It doesn't look a whole lot like the life of the characters of my stories. At any rate, we lived without a lot of money, under hard conditions. My father and my mother managed to survive the war. They bought a house with a lot of difficulty ten miles outside of London. I wasn't born there—the house I was born in was another one; it was located in the southwest of London. It was a very ordinary place. The childhood I had was very similar to that of any child from a working-class neighborhood after the war. I grew up in an era when England was coming out of the war and its effects, an era in which my parents made an effort to give us a certain security. I believe that that helped me to develop a sense of having a life and knowing that I could do something with this life, whatever that may be, so long as it was done with responsibility and conviction. In that, I believe, I had luck.

Vásquez: Some consider you a nineteenth-century novelist. In a formal sense, however, your novels are clearly modern—your debt to Faulkner is apparent—so critics must be referring to other aspects. Do you believe that there are clear nineteenth-century characteristics in your novels? Do you believe that that comment is referring to the writers who have influenced you?

Swift: I am a modern writer who doesn't worry too much about being one, who hasn't made an effort to acquire modernity. Of course, there are experimentations in modern literature that I don't share, and, of course, *Waterland*, to a large extent, deals with the nineteenth century. But I have never taken on the role of a contemporary; what's more, I believe that "contemporary" is a very dangerous word. The novel, because of its very essence, distances itself from the contemporary. When one takes two years to write a story, what was contemporary and current when he started the composition, is not so when it is ends. The novel, by its nature, tends to deny the day-to-day. Today and now are left to the journalist. The very word, "journalist," contains the idea of what corresponds to a day, to today. The novel must be atemporal. With regard to the thorny issue of influences, I must state a generality: A writer is influenced by everything he reads. But, in particular, writers that shape a young person are those who, at the right time, make him feel he would like to have written that novel, and not those who might have had more direct influence on his style. Those who make one say: I like the work of this writer a lot, and I want to do something on the same level. Therefore, I couldn't point out one in particular. But I couldn't *not* mention Isaac Babel, the magnificent writer of Russian stories, whose work looks nothing like mine. I can remember the first time I read his stories. It was right before I attended university; I must have been eighteen, or even seventeen. With fifty pounds in my pocket, I had decided to take a long trip. I travelled some three months through Greece, Turkey, and Eastern Europe. Even at that time I wanted to be a writer, and I remember having bought—I still had some money left—a copy of Isaac Babel's tales, in a Penguin edition. I read it with fascination. Ever since that moment, he has had a special place for me. But, you see, that happened at that time and in that place. It's perfectly possible that I might never have found Babel, and that would not have stopped my development as a writer. What is certain is that I read less every day. It has to be that way, I imagine. And I don't think too much about the writers who shaped me. I write with very few writers looking over my shoulder, and Isaac Babel is one of them.

Vásquez: And what can you tell me about Faulkner? One of the possible readings of *Last Orders* is that of an homage (merely a formal one, but a homage after all) to *As I Lay Dying*: A group of people take a trip to bury someone, and that trip is narrated by their alternating voices. Moreover, it deals with an archetypical novel more than any other novel you have written: Death as a rite of passage. Other critics have compared *Waterland* to *Absalom, Absalom!*, especially regarding the treatment of the past. This seems less evident to me, but it deserves comment.

Swift: I wouldn't speak of my novel as an homage to *As I Lay Dying*. In fact, I didn't think about Faulkner's novel when I was writing mine, even though Faulkner may be a writer I certainly admire. But this question is important because it leads us to another question: How does a novel begin? *Last Orders* didn't begin as literature, as another book, but rather as a feeling of writing about that situation: A person has died, there are some who remain living around that person. How do they handle that fact, how do they face it? What implications does it have? Which is also true of *As I Lay Dying*, but that's a situation that we all go through. And even though I haven't emphasized the fact, *Last Orders* was written right after my father's death. Of course my father was very different from the character of the butcher, Jack. So the real origin of that book is intensely personal. The last thing I thought about was how it resembled other books I read. I believe it's indeed an archetypical novel, and I'm happy that that's the way it is. What I am hoping it is, too, is a novel about very specific characters in a very specific place on a very specific day. But this must have a universal significance; at least, it's what one strives to achieve: to put on paper something that is very personal, very authentic, something that belongs to certain coordinates of time and place, and yet, so far as possible, it turns out to be valuable for all times and all places. I believe I strive to be archetypical, and this is probably the reason I throw out so much material: I write something, and then I feel like that something doesn't really touch a common nerve and that it is therefore useless. I am ambitious in that sense, which isn't the sense normally given to "ambition." Ambition almost always suggests the desire to do something vast, with grand ideas and all that. The more I write, and the older I get, the more I am convinced that it isn't like that. The artist's true ambition isn't in the magnitude of the ideas, but rather in the measure in which those ideas manage to touch that common and universal nerve. It has to do with something very direct. The magical thing is in taking an event with human content and showing why it is true for all time periods and eternally authentic. That's how it works, at least in my case. The greatest art for me is frequently in situations that seem to be small. Many times we think that a writer's ambition must be in taking great ingredients, but that doesn't necessarily lead to a work that stands the test of time. So, I believe my tendency is toward the inverse process. And that, I believe, shows up in *Last Orders*. It was a book that I turned the corner with. Now, when I was writing *Waterland*, I hadn't yet read *Absalom, Absalom!* However, I am aware that the sense of the past is strong in *Waterland*, just as it can be strong in several novels by Faulkner in the way that they have their characters react to it, to relate to it. Also, it's what you were mentioning before: the sense of place. That is also strong in Faulkner, but there are many other writers for whom the setting is as important as the figures that appear in that setting. If I thought about anyone at the time of writing *Waterland*, it was about Dickens.

Vásquez: In the Dickens of *Great Expectations*?
Swift: Of course. Even García Márquez, and all that Magical Realism, could be present then. There are sections of *Waterland* that are, in reality, very fantastical, in the sense of going beyond reality. Like the brewery, for example. Unlike everything I've done before or after, in *Waterland* there was that magical ingredient. But I believe I basically found myself alone with that book and its writing.

Vásquez: I'd like you to speak to me about the theme of history. It interests me for several reasons and, in short, as a leading thread in your books. There are several appearances of history's entry into your plots. Mircea Eliade said that what differentiates primitive man from civilized man is his interest in History, and your novels usually mark the passage of History (with a capital letter) to the stories (with a small letter). In *Waterland* it's said: "Man is the animal that tells stories."

Swift: First, let me comment on the Eliade quotation like this: It depends a bit on how we choose to define "modern" and "primitive." There was a time in human history when history was established in a form conscious of itself, if I may say so. I'm not sure when this was, and in my opinion, our sense of history is declining. When one watches the evolution of the last centuries, of the last five centuries, more or less, there always seems to be an important sense of history. I don't know if that can be said of the twentieth century. So I'm speaking about a phenomenon that may be very recent. I could be wrong, and this opinion might not be more than a consequence of my age, but I believe that the new generations, the generations that came after mine, do not have such a strong sense of history as mine. There is more a sense that life is now. For better or for worse, I grew up obsessed with history, even when I didn't realize it. I believe that that has a lot to do with having been born a little after the war and feeling that there was this gigantic event right behind me that affected so many ordinary lives. I have never managed to lose that sensation of immediacy, of proximity to the war. For me, that was a constant point of reference, and I do understand why it isn't for the new generations. What has the war got to do with them? So, where can they get a sense of history, if they ever do manage to get one, I don't know.

Is man the animal that tells stories? He must be, mustn't he? Other animals probably tell each other stories, who knows [he laughs]. By that, I mean that the interest in telling stories is part of our humanity, it's what makes us humans, and it's deeply rooted in our human nature. All of us respond to a sense of stories, and it's very difficult to conceive of a life without a sense of narration: a life that was only lived, without that narrative dimension, without being told. And now, to return to the question about what is primitive and what is modern, I believe our eagerness to tell stories is profoundly primitive in the sense that it isn't really explainable. It can't be analyzed, it's mysterious and magical. We talk about how good stories exert a spell, and I believe that that has a lot of truth. If one could go back in time, he would find that our most primitive ancestors would have a very strong necessity to tell stories. Stories awaken in us, even now, rather atavistic needs and responses. And just as stories can have relatively trivial purposes, like simply entertainment (and that isn't bad), at the other extreme they can rip out our hearts and our guts. They are a very basic need. When people say things like the book is dead, that it won't live much longer, that other things will take its place, I think, without considering the probable reason of their argument, that the need for stories will never die. If it dies, it will be because we are in effect dead.

Vásquez: The conflict that appears most often in your novels isn't between lovers or rivals, but rather between generations. Furthermore, except for the trivial fact that the narrator of *Waterland* was a teacher just like you were at some point, you seem to consciously deny writing about "what you know" in favor of "what others remember" or "what was lived before."

Swift: Now that I have written six novels, I can agree with you. The conflict between generations takes place in a lot in them. Why I feel attracted to these situations, I don't know. But it has to do with something that sounds true, because generations often have very strong conflicts between them. Like other conflicts, this one generates drama, and this is what I pursue with each one of my novels. Why does this interest me in particular? I suppose it's because I feel that I am a writer with long perspectives; and changes, the transformations that take place over long periods of time, interest me. The conflict between generations can usually be summed up like this: the inability to accept change to live in a world perceived by the eyes of another generation. Young people living in a world seen through old people and vice versa. Every generation thinks, at least at some point, that it's located outside history; and every generation learns, for better or for worse, that this isn't true. So, to reach a historical perspective is one of the results of maturity, and sometimes at the cost of much conflict. Some of my characters essentially learn this: to take a long and mature view of individual lives, to accept that they are not outside history, that everyone of us has our historical moment. This can be a comforting but also an unsettling thought.

Curiously, and even though the narrator of *Waterland* may be a teacher, there was not too much influence there. When I taught, I taught English, not History. I was never a History teacher. Plus, I taught at a very special level. It's difficult to define. I taught at institutions called "further education colleges," whose name sounds like a university, but in reality, they aren't. They are places where the people go who have failed in school, who have missed school years or who have not finished in order to try again. So, the level is very low. One could have students who had gone to school the year before and also students who were sixty or seventy years old. It was a very strange job. But I did it as a part-time job to finance my writing. I don't have an academic calling in reality, nor do I believe I was very good as a teacher, but it was something I could do part-time to earn money and be able to write. I did it for ten years; gradually, over time, I was cutting down on the time I dedicated to teaching. As I gained confidence in my writing, I cut back on my teaching time. Everything depended on the students: There were good classes and bad classes. So, I don't believe that any of that really made it into my writing.

To not write about what I know . . . I consider that stance a bit pigheaded, indeed. Of course, sometimes, in spite of myself, I write about things relatively close to my own experience. I don't agree with the view of the writer as someone who goes through life wondering if he can write about everything that's lived, ever in search of material. Life, contrary to what many writers think, is not there to be transformed into literature. I want to live my life, not exploit it for other purposes. There is, obviously, an unconscious element whereby one, in fact, digests his experience and uses it in his writing. But I emphasize unconscious. The important thing is to create, and if one goes through life saying "this is material I can use," he distances himself from creating, pure creating. Inventing something: That is what interests me. Finding something in my head and realizing I don't know where it comes from and recognizing it excites me, that it's become important to me: That is what matters. The task of a reporter bores me. One doesn't apply reporting to one's own life. But I know there are many writers—and many very good writers—who hold the opposite opinion: They believe that one should write about what they know, and they have written wonderful books based on that. I imagine, however, that a life's worth of experience can be used at most for two or three books. It's generally true that a writer's first novel is fed to a large extent by his own life and that sometimes that's his last novel and for that very reason. In reality, I am rather stubborn with regard to being anti-autobiographical. Obstinately stubborn.

Vásquez: Anti-autobiographical might have, however, some implications. One of them is the "sense of place," which could be absent. But that's not how it is: *Waterland* has an abundant sense of place. For me, the Fenland is as necessary to your novel as Yoknapatawpha is to Faulkner's (with the difference being that the Fens really exist).

Swift: There's a counter-argument to the anti-autobiographical genre: If you don't know, how can you pretend that you know? But I believe that is the magic, the mystery of writing. A form exists where the imagination manages to touch the truth or draw very near to the truth of things that are not known through experience. In part, that is what imagination is for. There are moments when I write about areas that are not in my life, and at one point, I feel something; I feel that I am right. It sounds terribly arrogant, but I feel that I am approaching the truth or that what I am writing is true. Even if I haven't been there, even if I haven't lived that. And there are other times when I try to do it, and I don't get it. I don't manage to reach the truth with what I'm writing. Then I throw it out. But sometimes I get it: I feel that I have been in places where I couldn't have been, and it's very exciting. *Waterland* was a lesson for me. Before that novel, setting hadn't been so important in my work. However, looking back I realize that my first novel, *Shuttlecock*, [sic] was full of a "sense of place." It was very localized. *Waterland* taught me, in a very obvious way, about place, about geography; it taught me the importance of those aspects. And now, without wanting to underscore that point too much, without wanting to put too much emphasis on it, I know that the location of a novel, its placement, is part of what a novel should offer. That's how it happens in *Last Orders*. The difference between both novels is that in *Last Orders*, I speak of places that are very close to me, that are very close to where I grew up. I didn't think about where I was going to set that novel; it was simply there. What is true is that the lives of the people take place in well-defined places. We can't, in reality, think about human experience without thinking about where it takes place. There is a type of novel in which there is no feeling of place, of course. In those novels, it's as if the actions took place in a room. A large room, but a room after all. And it turns out that they are not fulfilling; they don't seem true. Place is as important as what the people do, what they do when they are not in the middle of the drama, which is the theme of the novel. And work is important, too. There was, it's true, a period when the characters of a novel didn't do anything because they belonged to the social classes that didn't work. And again: One can read novels in which it seems like the characters don't do anything in life, and one wonders: What do these people do on a normal day? I believe that a novelist should know the response, even if it doesn't figure in his novel.

Vásquez: What can you say about the fictional autobiography? *Waterland* is the (partial) autobiography of a fictional character. But it's different from other fictional autobiographies, like *David Copperfield* or all the novels that came out of *Tristram Shandy*, inasmuch as the narrator of *Waterland* narrates from the moment of his crisis, instead of remembering the past crisis comfortably from the present.

Swift: Yes. What you're saying is very interesting. I have always believed that a story shouldn't simply happen. The writer must show the need for it to happen, why telling a story becomes absolutely necessary for a character. And that often happens at times of crisis: It's when one is in the middle of the crisis that one feels the urgency to tell what is happening. One wonders: How did I get here? What did I do wrong, how was I mistaken? And that implies looking back—almost automatically—in order to see what happened and to be able to tell the story. So, that's why my narrators are in the middle of their crises in one way or another. They are telling the story in an urgent way, if not to resolve their crises, to understand how they got to that point. Perhaps this is why I accept the view that a story can be therapeutic. We feel the need to get better, to comfort ourselves, and stories are there to do that. In this sense, the task of telling stories is a rather serious matter, isn't it? After all, that is—in broad strokes—what a psychiatrist does: He makes people tell their stories, tell their own story. On a professional and scientific level, it gets people to do something that they have been doing forever, for ages and ages. By this I don't mean to say, however, that stories make life better or that they can teach us how we should live in the future and thereby make the future better. But at least it helps us in our relationship with who we are, with what we have been. And it also helps us to understand our past and the way it has affected our present. It deals with very big, very important issues.

Vásquez: But there are no two people who tell their stories the same way. In the process of imposture, which is implicit in writing a novel, the writer can't discard that circumstance. You have chosen narrators very different from each other for your novels. What did you feel, for example, when you changed from a well-educated and polite narrator like Tom Crick in *Waterland* to a group of narrators of humble origin like those of *Last Orders*? Which leads me to another comment: In your novels, there is usually more than one narrator. The form in which they're arranged usually suggests that it's impossible to get to the bottom of the matter through the narration of a single person.

Swift: Well, *Last Orders* is . . . It's my best book, that's how I feel now, now that I can say so. It was a very liberating and a very refreshing book. It has to be said that it isn't written directly in colloquial language, but rather in a literary style that evokes colloquial language. So it is still a literary piece and not a recording of street speech. And when dealing with colloquial language, when facing characters that have not had a formal education, one could think that that would have been a problem, since it dealt with a limitation. And I found that it was the complete opposite. I didn't have, in reality, greater difficulties. I remember this in particular: I was starting the novel when I realized that I was going to write it in this language, and had I been more timid, I would have given myself a tap on the shoulder and asked myself: Are you sure about this? But I didn't do so because that language quickly became the language of the book. And at any rate, it deals with a language very close to me, since it was the language I heard all my life.

But the idea of a central, omniscient narrator has always been uncomfortable for me, one that unites all the pieces of the story. In some way, that is what my central narrators try to do. Particularly Tom Crick. They are constantly tripping over the attempt to put together a jigsaw puzzle. I have always written in first person; I like that feeling of an "I" that tells the story. Even when I have written in third person, that third person is very close to first. I suppose that that comes from certain philosophical convictions, like the fact that we are all locked up in our own ego; we all live in a world that we create and invent, a world private and different from everyone else's. We cannot abandon that compass. I believe I like first person because one has very immediate access to what is happening inside the character, and one, as author, is with the character in a way that is impossible when one writes in third person. These may be prejudices of mine, but third person gives me the feeling of being high above, of being superior to the character. When one writes in first person, he is with the character, at the same level. He is saying: I'm going along with him, I share the things he doesn't know, his limitations, his defects, I do not have a special insight in the ways he handles the world, I am just like any other, and the only thing I can do is share. And one, as author, shares the fate of the character. First person is an act of solidarity that one hopes to transmit to the reader: One hopes the reader also shares a character's fate. Because—getting back to the previous question—one of the important things about the novel is that it is created through collaboration. Every reader reads a different novel and is free to do so. He will read the novel the way he wants, bringing to the reading his own cultural baggage or nothing at all, his own expectations; he might set it down at any moment and pick it up later. It's something very democratic, if I'm permitted to use that term. This is how a novel differs from a film, where the image is definitive. Those who watch a movie could have different reactions and feelings, but they see essentially the same movie. I believe it's the main problem when a novel is adapted to cinema: The character is defined by the actor who represents him. In the end, what the writer wants is for the reader to feel that he has been there, to feel that recognition that the person who gave rise to what I'm reading (although there is no reason for the reader to remember that person in the course of the reading) is just like me and is telling me that he has the same confusion and the same limitations and the same questions that I do. The greatest literature is always an act of compassion.

The Critic Faces the Unhappy Author

Eileen Battersby / 2007

From *The Irish Times* (May 8, 2007) https://www.irishtimes.com/culture/the-critic-faces
-the-unhappy-author-1.1204873. Reprinted by permission of *The Irish Times*.

Graham Swift's latest book was a disappointment for Eileen Battersby, whose review led to a tense encounter with the author.

It was unexpected, all of it. After all, British writer Graham Swift, author of *Waterland*, one of the truly great novels not to win the Booker Prize, and author of *Last Orders*, one of the few truly great novels that did win it, is among the finest of contemporary novelists. When *The Light of Day* was published in 2003, some seven years after his Booker triumph, it confirmed that Swift was simply getting better and better.

In that wonderfully tender novel, George, an ex-policeman turned private detective, falls for a woman who hires him to track down her errant husband, a gynecologist. The woman is an academic and translator. George is the son of a High Street photographer, aware his own educational career was not overly impressive. There is an additional complication: George's client may or may not have killed her husband. So, as the narrative opens, she is serving time in prison.

Swift's new novel, *Tomorrow*, also has a central narrator. Paula, confidently approaching fifty, is happily married to Mike and they have sixteen-year-old twins, a boy and a girl. It is a midsummer night and she is unable to sleep because the next day could change all of their lives. It could be a disaster, it may not be. But either way, nothing will be the same. A new novel from Graham Swift, his first in four years, is significant. *The Irish Times* agreed to interview him, even before the new novel had arrived in Ireland, never mind been read.

So Paula tells her story and that of her marriage and makes no secret of the nature of the revelation. She lies in bed beside her sleeping husband, aware that the next day will see her children discovering that the man who has reared them and loved them, and indeed once risked his life to save them, is not their father. Initially, there is the suggestion of either an affair or merely a desperate attempt to become pregnant.

It should be compelling and human, but Paula the narrator proved too cool and complacent for me, and never fully convinces, and I pointed this out in the review I wrote of the book. Nor did I much like her sexual candor in an imaginary conversation she is directing at her children. Graham Swift read the review and was given the option to decline the interview but decided to carry on with it. I don't know why he bothered—we didn't have an interview, because he was only interested in correcting the review. But perhaps the encounter has some value as a cautionary tale? Reviewers are useful—when they write favorably.

Over the years, since the publication of *Waterland*, I have reviewed each of Swift's novels, each one favorably. Having read his work, and twice interviewed him, I consider him one of the most consistently interesting fiction writers. Throughout his career, which began when his first two novels, *The Sweet-Shop Owner* and *Shuttlecock*, as well as a collection of stories, *Learning To Swim*, earned his place in *Granta*'s 1983 Best of the Young British Novelists list, he has been a major presence, always there—if overshadowed by the linguistic dazzle and satiric comedy of Martin Amis. Swift, Amis and Ian McEwan, as well as Salman Rushdie, Pat Barker, Kazuo Ishiguro, Julian Barnes and William Boyd all featured in that class of 1983.

Swift has always asked questions without presuming to offer answers. *Waterland*, his third novel, remains a major achievement, and when people ask how it could have possibly failed to win the 1983 Booker Prize, there is a logical explanation—he had the bad luck to come up against probably the finest novel ever to win, J. M. Coetzee's *Life & Times of Michael K*. In 1992, Swift published another impressive work, *Ever After*, one of the most underrated contemporary British novels.

Then flash forward to early 1996 and *Last Orders*, a colorful odyssey through the lives of a small group of Londoners who find themselves part of a pilgrimage when they are entrusted with the ashes of a mutual friend, Jack Dodds. On publication, it was destined for the Booker. It was also the book that showed how well Swift, the writer of ideas, could use voice. Yet just as voice proved the defining strength of *Last Orders* and *The Light of Day*, it does not succeed in *Tomorrow*, because Paula never lives off the page—or at least she didn't for me.

Graham Swift rises from his seat and makes it clear from the outset that he is not pleased. "I don't know how we are going to do this interview as that review you wrote may . . . was . . . well, may have been about another book. You said Paula was cold, she is not. She is warm and loving and really funny—but you missed that. I've never been in this position before."

I have. I can remember arriving for an interview with Nadine Gordimer. "Oh," she said, "I didn't realize it was you. I was very pleased with your review," she smiled at me, and then shrewdly announced to her publicist: "I've already had an excellent review from her—I don't need an interview in the same paper, I will go for a nap." Reviews, it seems, are about immediate market-place publicity, not literary criticism.

Swift is as disappointed with my review as I was with the book. He falls silent, as he will several times over the duration of the long hour of an interview that felt more like a college tutorial—although I always remember them as being enjoyable.

"I can't understand how you failed to see my book as I meant it," Swift continues. At the beginning of his career, Swift was a teacher and it is the disappointed teacher, not the writer, who is present. Early on, I put to Swift that he can have the last word in the interview as it appears on the page—and that word or sentence will be his telling me "go read the book again." He seems to agree.

It is the first time I have ever had a major international novelist quote lines from my review back to me. "You said she is not 'sympathetic'; she is, she loves her husband and her children. She is happy in her life. You seem to have a problem with the fact that she is middle class. You like George, maybe you only like underdogs?" Is he commenting on my approach to fiction in general? Or merely to the book in question? I don't have a problem with middle-class characters and I don't only relate to underdogs, but I do know that I don't much warm to "cool and complacent," which is how Paula struck me, so perhaps Swift has a point.

Swift also points out that he can't "write the same book every time." I was not suggesting that he did. A middle-aged man and a young woman sitting across from us appear to be listening. It is embarrassing. I think I look like an undercover agent who let the quarry slip away and is now being ticked off by an outraged superior.

The tea is getting cold—the tea is cold.

"No bad review ever torpedoed a novel. An unfavorable notice may stop a theater run, or discourage people going to a movie, but a book review doesn't have that power," I point out. "Your readers will read this book. Had my review been written by someone else, I would still read this novel as

I have read all of your books." Trying to deflect the interview away from
Tomorrow and back to his other books fails.

"I don't want to talk about my other books, I am here to talk about my
new one, the one you have thrashed. I just can't understand it, how you
could fail to like Paula. I love her."

Obviously, he is pleased with this novel. "I am proud of and pleased with
all my books, just as I am proud and pleased with this one, the book that
you have misunderstood. I can't understand how an intelligent critic has got
something so wrong."

Not for an instant do I feel that I am St. Sebastian-like, taking all the
arrows that outraged novelists want to direct at wayward reviewers; instead,
I am genuinely surprised that an experienced and established novelist is
reacting in such a way. I also feel that the review is being as misrepresented
by his reaction as he feels his novel has been. Not for the first time in this
meeting (one can hardly call it an interview), I remind him that I admire his
other books, but just don't happen to like this one.

"I don't know why you don't. This is a book about love, love, love. Paula
loves her children; Paula loves her husband."

Muted exasperation fuels my reflex reply. "Then why does she have
that affair with the vet?" There seems to have been more than a desperate
attempt to become pregnant. He agrees ("That was an experiment"), but still
he stresses the love and Paula's love. Paternity is one of the big themes of the
book, although Swift cuts across, "there are lots of themes, especially love."

It seems unfair that Mike's role as a father could be diminished by a
medical technicality; after all, he has raised them. In the strongest scene,
a holiday swimming drama almost ends in tragedy, but for Mike's courage.
"Oh yes," says Swift drily, "I'm glad you liked that bit." When he says "love is
keeping her awake. She is worried about Mike," I suggest that her sleepless-
ness may also be due to her unease over being about to spend her twenty-
fifth wedding anniversary night in the same hotel room in which she had
had her fling with the vet.

But nothing exists except for the review, which was not a hasty slam job,
just a disappointed response to a book I couldn't believe. Perhaps had the
book been written thirty years ago, or fifty years, the method of conception
may have been more shocking. I contend Mike is still the father; a test tube
can't compete with a man with a face. Does Swift have children? "No, by
choice," he says. As he rises and half-heartedly offers his hand, side on as he
moves away, I remind him that he has the final word. So here I am conclud-
ing as agreed: the novelist says: "Read the book again."

An Interview with Graham Swift

Stef Craps / 2008

Originally published in *Contemporary Literature* (2009) 50.4: 637–61.
© 2009 by the Board of Regents of the University of Wisconsin System.
Reprinted by permission of the University of Wisconsin Press.

Graham Swift is one of the most successful and respected novelists writing in contemporary Britain. Since 1980 he has published eight novels, a collection of short stories, and a nonfiction book. His work has garnered critical acclaim and literary prizes, and it has won a large and appreciative audience throughout the English-speaking world and beyond. His most celebrated books are *Waterland*, from 1983, which is widely considered a modern classic, and *Last Orders*, which was awarded the prestigious Booker Prize in 1996. Both novels have also been made into films. His latest novel, *Tomorrow*, came out in 2007.

Swift belongs to a generation of talented novelists born around the middle of the twentieth century—including Peter Ackroyd, Martin Amis, Julian Barnes, Kazuo Ishiguro, and Salman Rushdie—who, as they came to prominence in the late 1970s and early 1980s, were seen to represent a new wave in British fiction. However, Swift has never allied himself with any literary school or movement, and his work defies easy categorization. For example, it seems too invested in the traditional concerns of the English novel (like exploration of character and storytelling) to warrant the label "postmodern," which can be more readily applied to many of his peers, yet too self-conscious and formally sophisticated to fit comfortably under the rubric of realism.

With fellow novelists Pat Barker, Kazuo Ishiguro, and Caryl Phillips, though, Swift shares an evident and abiding preoccupation with issues of trauma, memory, and recovery. His protagonists—mostly first-person narrators—tend to be humble, unheroic, vulnerable elderly men who are forced by a crisis situation in their personal lives to face up to an often traumatic individual and collective past. They feel the slipping away of the foundations upon which they, and the society to which they belong, have built their existence, and by means of which they have sought to keep the trauma at bay. The question that they now face is how to respond to this situation of unsettlement and perplexity—whether to hide or flee from it or to try and engage with it in a meaningful way. While denial is shown to have catastrophic consequences, Swift's work also raises the possibility that the process of working through trauma might create the conditions for a viable alternative *modus vivendi* based on openness to and respect for otherness.

This interview was conducted in the dining room of a beautiful and delicately restored Victorian pub in the South London suburb of Wandsworth, near where the author lives, on 31 January 2008. I had first met Swift some two months earlier at a conference in Liège, Belgium, where he gave a keynote address that I had been asked to introduce. The text of this lecture, titled "I Do Like to Be beside the Seaside: The Place of Place in Fiction," was to find its way into *Making an Elephant: Writing from Within*, the nonfiction book published in 2009 which he was then working on. The writing of this new book, which involved revisiting and reworking several older pieces, put him in a retrospective mood, as did the introduction for a special anniversary edition of *Waterland* on which he was then about to start and which he had completed by the time we met again on the other side of the English Channel. The moment seemed right, therefore, for an interview that would focus not only on his most recent novel but also on recurrent concerns and evolutions across his work—an interview, in other words, that would take stock of where Swift stands as a writer twenty-five years on from *Waterland*.

Q: At your publisher's request, you have written an introduction for the twenty-fifth anniversary edition of *Waterland* that will be coming out later this year. Am I right to assume that you have mixed feelings about this project? After all, *Waterland* is a book that has obviously brought you fame and, I hope, fortune, but whose huge reputation has also, to some extent, come to overshadow all your later work, with the possible exception of *Last Orders*; and now with this new edition coming out, it will be getting even more attention than it already did. Would it be fair to say that you have a love/hate relationship with this novel?
A: I think that's a little extreme. I do have a mixture of feelings, as you put it. But even that phrasing suggests I might be more uncomfortable than I am. I'm actually perfectly happy to be going back to that book now. It's nice

that my publishers want to make a thing about its twenty-fifth anniversary. But there was a sort of middle period when that novel did dominate people's impression of me. On the one hand, I was happy, like any author should be happy, that my name could be linked with at least one of my books. After all, there are many authors for whom that doesn't happen. So I had become "the author of *Waterland*," and in one sense that label was not a bad thing, but it started to hang around my neck a little. The more I produced after *Waterland*, the more I felt this to be the case. Until, I would say, *Last Orders*, which had a comparable success, in some ways a greater success, winning the Booker Prize and so on. For me, that virtually solved the difficulty. So now, with two novels after *Last Orders*, I feel I can quite comfortably go back to *Waterland* in this way and see what I feel about it.

Q: Would you say that *Waterland* is as relevant to the world today as it was to the world twenty-five years ago? Does it still speak to contemporary concerns?
A: Yes, it does. In fact, this is one of those things that, coming back to it now and writing an introduction for it, I actually address. What I've found is that it feels as relevant now as then. Not just because it deals, I hope, with some timeless things that are always relevant, but because even some things that seem to date the novel have their equivalents now. It was published in 1983, but it looks back to the late 1970s. It looks back to that time very much still within the cold war, and to the prevailing fear—I have a direct memory of it—of some nuclear Armageddon. Everyone felt it, but certainly young people of school age. Their futures were shadowed by this very real possibility. That fear is very much part of the book, and you could say that it's all gone now, it went with the end of the cold war. But there are clearly other very apocalyptic notions around, which have taken the place, as it were, of that fear.

Q: I assume you're thinking of terrorism, global warming, and so on?
A: Terrorism, climate change, global warming: all those obvious things, which, I would say, exercise the minds of young people, students, just as much as the nuclear thing would have troubled students back then. So on the one hand, I can see how the novel dates, like any novel dates. It belongs to the period of its writing, the period it refers to. But in another sense, I was struck by how it relates to the present day. Then again, you could take some of its central metaphors, the whole metaphor of the Fens—not that the Fens are just a metaphor—as embodying a process of history, human endeavor, an elemental struggle, preserving the land against water and

flooding: all that seems to me to work just as well now and even to have certain applications, implications, that it might not have had then.

Q: Such as?
A: Well, I think you could say that the geographical quality of that metaphor is even more pertinent now, because, for one thing, we're getting more floods. This country, many countries are getting more floods. The land that we live on is more physically under threat now in most parts of the world. So a landscape that embodies that constant threat and that constant need for preservation has all the more resonance now.

Q: Right, definitely. But that's on the literal level still: what about the metaphorical level?
A: But I think the literal and the metaphorical really merge with each other. The physical process of preserving territory blends with the historical process of how we progress or not, how we survive, how we hold on, not just to physical and geographical things, but to civilization itself, how we face the future, how we acknowledge the past, how we use the past to face the future. All those things are implicit in the business of land reclamation. One thing that struck me, going back to the book, was how wonderful it was that at some point in the evolution of the novel I hit upon the Fens as my setting, this region that can look so flat and empty, yet which proved so rich in significance. It was a key moment in the genesis of the novel. It seems to me now that the metaphorical dimension is virtually limitless. You can make it work in all kinds of human dilemmas, in all kinds of historical situations, including those the world is in right now.

Q: I agree. It seems to me that *Waterland* offers a critique of ideological mystification. A central point that it makes is that redemptive ideologies more often lead to catastrophe than to salvation. As a kind of antidote, Tom Crick, the narrator of the novel, promotes the cultivation of curiosity. He champions a model of progress—progress as land reclamation—that requires a sustained commitment to the questioning of grand narratives which distort a complex reality.
A: Yes. Something very prosaic and, to use a word that the novel uses and dwells on, phlegmatic. Something undramatic, unsensational, very much not to do with moments that are going to change things overnight— revolutionary moments. It's very skeptical.

Q: Exactly. These concerns were obviously very relevant in the early 1980s, when the Cold War—which was basically about two opposing redemptive ideologies coming into conflict—was still in full swing and the Falklands War, Britain's then latest imperial venture, was still fresh in people's memories. But they are also relevant, it seems to me, to our own era, in which we are still reeling from two disastrous wars, in Iraq and Afghanistan, which were partly justified on the grounds of spreading freedom and democracy throughout the world—another ideological fantasy, perhaps, in need of debunking.

A: Well, one might have to be a little bit careful here with exact chronology. *Waterland* was published in 1983, after the Falklands, but it was being written before that. The writing of it really didn't, in any effective way, register that event, though it was referred to in my next book, *Out of This World*. It would be a mistake, because *Waterland* was published in 1983, to see it as immediately incorporating things that occurred in 1982, 1983. As I say, it looks back to the 1970s. But more broadly, what you suggest is true. I wrote *Waterland*, which, among other things, deals with nostalgic, grandiose notions about British power, empire, influence in the world, and then, lo and behold, there was this event which made a huge appeal to that kind of emotion. Looking back now, I think there was a curious innocence to the Falklands episode, grotesque though it was. It was possible to say that there was a justification for it. That's to say, there were those British citizens, living in those islands far away on the other side of the world, and they were about to be kicked out by a foreign power. Absurd though it was, you could argue that the British government had no choice but to do what it did, assuming it couldn't solve the problem diplomatically. That little, questionable war had a kind of genuineness to it. The wars that we're talking about now are not like that. They have no innocence—innocence is not the right word anyway, in connection with war, but they absolutely don't. While I remember feeling skeptical and uncomfortable about the Falklands, I don't think I ever felt about it the real sense of shame that I feel now about how my country is involved in Iraq. It's shameful. My nation is besmirched by it in a way that I don't think was the case with the Falklands. So we've moved on, or rather moved back, in a pretty appalling way. I guess that's a real difference about the climate now—let's forget the climate in the literal sense. The moral climate in this country now involves a feeling of shame. What is there to be proud about? I don't think that was true in the 1970s or 1980s, for all the troubles that we had then, even including Northern Ireland. Even Northern Ireland didn't produce the underlying sense of shame that exists now.

Q: It's interesting to hear you talk about politics . . .
A: I seem to be doing so, yes. I don't very often do that.

Q: Indeed. Which brings me to my next question. Do you think that writers have a political responsibility? I'm asking this because many other British writers, especially since 9/11, seem to believe this to be the case: Martin Amis, David Hare, Ian McEwan, Harold Pinter, Salman Rushdie, and so on. However, in marked contrast to these writers, you have so far refrained from making public pronouncements on burning political issues such as the rise of Islamic fundamentalism or the war in Iraq.
A: Which I wouldn't want to do. I would say that it's not me. I'd be extremely hesitant, at least, about doing that. And insofar as I have been asked and invited to do that, I have always basically said no. I don't think that's the role of a writer, in fact. There's a great tendency to think that if a person has some sort of expertise or mark in one field, they're therefore good at everything else. So a writer with a reputation should therefore be able to act as a kind of leader of opinion on any number of subjects. I think that's a very false assumption. I find it actually often rather embarrassing when writers, as it were, sound off in the press and media about this or that subject, which is not their real purpose.

Q: I'm reminded of your essay "Looking for Jiří Wolf," published in *Granta* in 1990, in which you reflect on the uneasy relationship between aesthetics and politics. You describe your encounters with a number of dissident writers from the former Czechoslovakia who lived and worked under communism. From reading this piece, I got the impression that you shared the "secret wish" expressed by one of them not to be involved in politics, but that you also appreciated how under certain circumstances it becomes imperative for a writer to speak out and take a stand. Have you ever felt that need yourself?
A: No. I can conceive of finding myself in a situation which, as it were, demanded that I should speak out, but I don't think such a situation has actually occurred in this country.

Q: So what would it take for you to feel the need to speak out?
A: I think I'm talking about radical and extreme political changes which would seriously affect freedom. I'm talking about the kind of thing, in other words, that would have pertained in Czechoslovakia and many other countries at the time I wrote that piece.

Q: Also in contrast to quite a few other writers, you don't deal with the great dramatic events of the early twenty-first century in your recent fictional work. In fact, both *Tomorrow* and *The Light of Day* are set in the 1990s—that is, in the pre-9/11 era.

A: I've often said, a little teasingly, that I don't believe in contemporary fiction. I don't think there is such a thing as contemporary fiction. The great strength of fiction is that it isn't and cannot be contemporary, because of the time it takes to write. If I was going to write a contemporary novel about now, today, late January 2008, that novel would take me—being me—at least a couple of years, by which time it would, in that sense, be out of date. Fiction has to handle time and change in a longer way. I think the contemporary area belongs to journalism. It's the task of journalists to write about now, today: that's what "journal" means. Novelists do something else. I think the notion a lot of novelists have—maybe young novelists more than older novelists—that they've got to be contemporary all the time, have got to put in contemporary references, have got to demonstrate that they are responding to the world now can be misguided. What the novel can do is to put a period, a long period of time, in perspective, so that the great novel—if there's going to be one—about the war in Iraq, about my country in the beginning of the twenty-first century, may well not happen for another ten, fifteen years. It will take that process of historical ingestion, and anyway it will take the long process that it takes to write a novel. You can't do it just like that. September 11 particularly has made some writers feel, "God, this is such an inescapable, such a huge traumatic event, with the world's eyes upon it, that I must write about it, I must produce my 9/11 response in some form." Doing that, with conscious effort and will, has landed some writers in trouble. I don't think it works like that. Again, it's journalists who do that work. One big change that has occurred in my lifetime in the world of writing is an ever-increasing confusion of the roles of the journalist and of the fiction writer—sometimes quite literally, because there are many fiction writers who, I think, would like to be journalists, or indeed who were once journalists, and vice versa. There's been a growing lack of distinction between the two activities, but I think there's a fundamental distinction, an important distinction.

Q: You are currently working on your first-ever nonfiction book. Who or what gave you the idea for it? I'm intrigued, because in the past you have only very rarely written nonfictional prose; in fact, you've been remarkably single-minded in your dedication to the art of the novel.

A: This book, which is probably going to be published next year, sprang up partly just as a matter of opportunity. I had finished *Tomorrow*, although I was still seeing that book through to publication. I was in the mood a writer can be in after finishing a book: part of you wants just to do nothing, part of you is wondering what you will do next, part of you is looking for a change. It began to strike me that I should have a look at some pieces I'd written a long time ago, like the Jiří Wolf piece, and see if I couldn't put together a book of such pieces, with some new things added. Such an opportunity—especially for a writer like me, where there haven't been many such pieces—is only going to happen once. I suppose I recognized I'd reached a point in my writing life where I could do this, where there would be enough material to make this book. But that was only the beginning, because, as I thought about it, I very much wanted this book, if it was going to happen, to be not like the average book that novelists can produce in this way—that's to say, just a collection of pieces, a bundle of items. I wanted it to have a real shape, with linking pieces that would be specially written. Those links are often autobiographical ones, or to do with the personal side of writing, or my sense—so far as it goes—of being in a community of writers. I mean, my writer friends—there's a lot about my writer friends. It's a personal book, a very refreshing book for me to be working on. But I'm convinced that it's a total one-off. I have no idea how it will be received.

Q: It seems to me that autobiographical writing is another new departure for you. In the past you've always said that you dislike the notion that writers should write from their own experience, about what they know.
A: Well, in fact, that is the starting point for the book. I've written a short introduction which makes that very point, that as a fiction writer I'm very much nonautobiographical. I've often made a point of this when I've spoken about my work. I want to turn that around with this book and, as it were, step into the foreground for once, say things about me, what it feels like to be a writer, things about certain periods in my life which were important for my writing. I'm putting myself in front of the reader, in the full knowledge that normally I don't do this. I hope this might have a certain appeal, but we'll see.

Q: I'd like to talk about your development as a writer. Critics can't seem to make up their minds about the nature of the relationship between your novels. MacDonald Harris, for example, has described your oeuvre as "a familiar family of novels that resemble one another like siblings who have, perhaps, an odd marital infidelity or two in their heritage"; John Banville, on the other hand, has said that your novels "differ greatly from one another; indeed, were it not for the evidence of his name on the title page, one might think that all six of them had been written by different hands." Could you perhaps adjudicate between them?

A: I'm quite pleased by the contradiction, because insofar as I think about this at all, I think that both things are true. And I think it's healthy that both things are true. There is a way in which, after you've written a number of books, you can't really fail to recognize that there are certain things you keep coming back to. There is a core of concerns, which I wouldn't really be able to define, but it's always going to be there in anything I do. So, too, the reader knows there's going to be that recognizable element: "This is a Graham Swift novel." That is going on at the same time as every novel is in some way a new departure, it's something different. I think my work so far manifests that—sometimes quite strikingly. Just take the contrast between, say, *Ever After* and *Last Orders*. Both have, at their core, concerns that will always feature in my writing, but in another sense they're vastly different. The one has this highly educated character in a very educated setting; the other has these people who are talking a totally different language, in a completely different world. Or if you were to take the contrast between either of those novels and my most recent one, *Tomorrow*, again there's a huge change of milieu, of where the characters are coming from. So I think there's diversity and range in my work. And quite right, too, because that's one of the things you want to do as a novelist: you want to have range.

Q: Do you also see an evolution of your work, in linear terms?
A: I'm less sure about that. I don't mean that there may not be such a thing, but I'm not sure that I'm able to draw conclusions.

Q: Okay, let me try. Take the sequence of *The Sweet-Shop Owner*, *Ever After*, and *The Light of Day*. To some extent, I think, *Ever After* and *The Light of Day* can be seen as rewritings of *The Sweet-Shop Owner*, which in a sense take things one or two steps further. In some ways, *Ever After* begins where *The Sweet-Shop Owner* leaves off. *The Sweet-Shop Owner* ends with a suicide; *Ever After* starts with a failed suicide. The protagonist of *The Sweet-Shop Owner* appears to be stuck in a state of incomprehension and frustration with no possibility of redemption this side of the grave; *Ever After*, on the other hand, can be read as a prolonged, tortuous attempt by the narrator to break free from the unreflective, narcissistic way of life that led up to

his desperate act and to move toward a more viable and sustainable ethos. It seems to me that *The Light of Day* carries this process still further. It's a novel that refers back to *The Sweet-Shop Owner* even more explicitly than *Ever After*. In both *The Light of Day* and *The Sweet-Shop Owner*, the action takes place on a bright and sunny day, in a rigorously circumscribed London setting; the protagonist runs a business on the main shopping street, used to be a poor student, and does "homework" for the woman he loves; and so on and so forth. However, the differences are even more striking. *The Sweet-Shop Owner* is a very bleak and pessimistic novel, in which the protagonist is devastated at being abandoned by his daughter; in *The Light of Day*, however, the daughter miraculously comes back. There is a lot of love in *The Light of Day*, whereas love is almost unthinkable in *The Sweet-Shop Owner*.
A: Yes, in one sense it's a pretty loveless book.

Q: It's also significant, I think, that the crisis situation in *The Light of Day*— the protagonist's sacking from the police force, his divorce from his wife— does not occur in the narrative present, as is usually the case in your work, but years earlier. George has been given a new chance in life, and he's facing the realistic prospect of a new love relationship. I'm inclined to see this difference as evidence of a kind of linear evolution, from an emphasis on denial and evasion in your early work, through an intense preoccupation with the demands of trauma in your "middle-period" novels, to an embrace of renewal and regeneration in your latest novels. Does that make any sense to you?
A: Well, I think a lot of the things that you have said I certainly recognize. For example, the echoes that exist in *The Light of Day* with my first novel, *The Sweet-Shop Owner*. Those echoes have occurred to me, but only after I'd finished *The Light of Day*. During the writing of that novel, I was immersed in the world of that novel, and I certainly wasn't pausing to think, "Oh, I have a character here who has a position on a high street, who is making these very localized but resonant journeys in the course of a short period, like Willy Chapman in *The Sweet-Shop Owner*." I didn't really think of that at the time. It may sound odd that I shouldn't have done, but it just shows you how engrossed you are in the individual thing you're working on. But having written the novel, I can see that. And I can see that such things are examples of what I was talking about earlier. You write six, seven, eight novels, and you start to see certain things recurring, certain things you're not going to get away from. There's a way in which, though you write several novels, you may even be working on the same, single novel, as it were, with each one.

The linear thing, though, is tricky. I really think it's an interpretive thing. If you were to take George in *The Light of Day* and Willy in *The Sweet-Shop Owner*, yes, you could say that for George there is redemption, for Willy not much redemption, only a kind of ultimate settling of accounts, a death which is a form of suicide. But I'm not sure that the difference between the two characters represents some evolution or conscious direction. They're just two different characters. It's a matter of interpretation, anyway. When I write, I'm very much not an interpreter. I don't wish to be one stage ahead of my characters, interpreting what they're doing with hindsight, and certainly not with some kind of overall plan. Another way of putting this is to say that I actually have as much rapport, empathy, sympathy, connection with Willy Chapman as I have with George. Both of those characters are still as present and as real for me as they were at the particular times I created them and wrote about them.

I don't grade them morally, ethically. I don't wish to say that one was more successful than the other. All of that is precluded by the need to be as empathetic as I can be. While I'm not an autobiographical writer, while neither of those characters is me, I want to be as close as I can possibly get to my characters, and I want my readers to be as close as they can possibly get to my characters. And that closeness is almost more important to me than any form of interpretation. One of my articles of faith as a novelist is that you are suspending judgment, you are not saying that this is better than that. You're putting sympathy and compassion before moral judgment— which is not the same as saying there is no moral dimension to writing, far from it. I think there is a moral dimension, but it's a moral dimension which is governed by empathy, compassion, and a preparedness to suspend easy judgment on anyone who features in the story. If I have developed as a writer, I hope that I've developed in accordance with that article of faith.

Q: Let's stay with this article of faith for a while. In "Throwing Off Our Inhibitions," a feature published in *The Times* in 1988, you wrote, "the fundamental task of literature is to enable us to enter, imaginatively, experiences *other* than our own." However, the kinds of characters peopling your books fall within a rather limited range in terms of racial, gender, and class background: all of your protagonists so far have been white and heterosexual, and most of them male and middle class or upper lower-class. I'm not suggesting that you "are" any of your characters, but in these respects, at least, they don't seem to be all that far removed from you or from your own experience. Or would you say that such social markers are irrelevant when it comes to understanding what it is like to be someone else, that any "someone else" will do?

A: I think they're secondary, I think they're very secondary. I'm not sure that I agree with you, in one sense, that I am so close to the range of characters I've written about. I mean, it may sound a bit obvious and simplistic, but I've never been a detective, I've never been a butcher, I've never been a woman who works in the fine-art world, that sort of thing. The difference between any two people, however seemingly alike they may be, however seemingly they may belong to the same socio-economic bracket, is vast. The difference between one unique individual and another unique individual is a unique difference. It's as vast as that. So I think the way that we group people, as though they are like each other, is often highly suspect in itself. Merely to inhabit, so to speak, another person, as a writer or as a reader, is to cross a huge gulf, and to assume that certain people would not be that different from you, the reader or the writer, would be superficial and to disrespect their unique individuality. There's a kind of politically correct notion that a novelist ought to have all the right ingredients in the recipe, ought to include people with ethnic differences, different sexual proclivities, different social backgrounds—that that is almost of itself the stuff of any novel. I think that's, frankly, silly. It's not like that. The big jump, the big gap, is just the gap between any two people.

Q: As I'm sure you're aware, accusations of political incorrectness have in fact been leveled at your work. Your frequent reliance on white, male, and middle-class protagonists has been taken to imply—and I'm not saying I agree with this—a narrow and conservative outlook, a refusal to engage with feminist issues and with the multicultural reality of contemporary society. I'm thinking particularly of criticisms that have been made of *Last Orders*. One critic, for example, used the words "narrow-minded," "smug," and "parochial" in this connection.

A: Well, I wonder who the narrow-minded one really was.

Q: Fair enough. If you will allow me, I'd like to pursue a little further this question of the sympathetic imagination, which you say you have faith in and which you view as a force for good. I'm wondering whether the picture isn't more complex than that. Insofar as the imagination is a reproductive, mimetic faculty, isn't there a danger that instead of welcoming otherness into the world, it only pretends to do that, while what it's actually doing is endlessly reproducing the self?

A: I think you could say there is good and bad imagination. Imagination can be used well, or misused, or, indeed, neglected. But as a creative writer, as a writer of made-up, fictional worlds, I absolutely have to trust in and believe in the imagination. Imagination is the driving force of it all, and I set enormous store by it. It has a moral dimension. If we can imagine ourselves into the lives of others, that clearly has a moral effect. What else is morality based on than the ability to be not just a solipsistic unit but to imagine what it's like to be someone else? That's the beginning of morality. So the imagination is fundamentally important for me in that way, and I almost instinctively recoil from a notion that suspects the imagination. As I say, it can be misused, but I do think it's essentially one of the great forces of life, something that makes it possible better to enjoy or better to endure life. That's not me, that's Dr. Johnson. There may well be circumstances in which the imagination operates in a sort of corrupt way, but I think they're the exceptions and the peculiarities rather than the main thing. And I feel confident that my own imagination isn't corrupt, if I can put it like that.

Q: Sure. Let's talk about the settings of your novels. It has often been noted that your novels have a great sense of place. Rather than being a merely accidental backdrop, the setting has a crucial role in your writing, as it actively interferes with the human drama played out in it. Many of your novels are set in specific South London suburbs—Clapham in *Shuttlecock*, Lewisham and Greenwich in *Waterland*, Bermondsey in *Last Orders*, Chislehurst and Wimbledon in *The Light of Day*, and Putney in *Tomorrow*— or in quiet provincial backwaters like the East Anglian Fens in *Waterland* and the West Country in *Ever After*. Moreover, they seldom venture beyond English borders. In fact, the only novels with a slightly more international setting that come to mind are *Shuttlecock*, *Out of This World*, and *Last Orders*, some parts of which are set in France, Greece, the United States, and Egypt. Both the marginality and the Englishness of your settings make your work stand out. What is it that draws you to these suburban or provincial English settings?

A: I think it is their locality; it is the localness. Localness is the key. If you are going to write about things which are in fact universal and timeless, then the way to do it is through the focus of the local. If, on the other hand, you say, as it were, "Hey, look, I'm now being universal and global and big, because my book has obviously big things in it and it is set in half a dozen different international localities"—well, that often turns out to be rather pretentious. Some novels I have read which do that sort of thing have ceased to interest me quite quickly. I think you have to begin where we all begin, which is with our indisputably local sense of life and experience. However "global" we like to think we've become, it remains true that life is about our little corner, our little nook, our little niche, our little territory. It's a small world, but that small world opens up to the big world, and that's simply the way I go about things. For me, the London suburbs, for example, are as rich a field as anywhere, as rich a beginning to a novel as any beginning.

Q: So you don't see any tension between the familiarity of the places that you typically write about and your "maxim," as you called it in "Throwing Off Our Inhibitions," that novelists should not write from their own experience? Would you say, perhaps, that these familiar places are not so familiar as they seem?
A: They start by being familiar, but they become less familiar. That's one of the thrills I look for—discovering the extraordinary in the ordinary. That's the direction I like to go in. I can see that there would appear to be a contradiction between my saying, "Don't be autobiographical, don't write about what you know," and my producing several novels which are set very close to home. However, I would come back to two things. Firstly, there's that huge difference between one person and another, so that even if the physical territory is superficially familiar, you are entering the unique inner worlds of your characters. Secondly, I think the familiar simply can be strange. The London suburbs, once you look beneath their surface, can be very strange. That paradox attracts me. I think writers perhaps have a special alertness for the strangeness we can all encounter in ordinary life. You walk into a familiar room, a familiar place, you go down a familiar street, but there's a strangeness in the air, you sense it. What's going on here? That's how a lot of stories begin.

Q: I'd like to talk about *Tomorrow* for a while. *Tomorrow* marks the first time that you have chosen a woman to be the only narrator of a novel, though there were already speaking parts for not-so-minor female characters in *The Sweet-Shop Owner*, *Out of This World*, and *Last Orders*. I'm wondering what made you decide to narrate this book entirely in the voice of Paula, rather than (also) in that of her male partner, Mike, who is sound asleep beside her. After all, Mike appears to be in deeper trouble than Paula is, as he is in greater danger of losing his children. Does this not make him at least as qualified to take on the task of narrating the story, or some parts of it, as his wife?
A: I think what made me decide was a fair amount of reflection. I certainly gave consideration to who was going to be telling the story, and, of course,

there was the possibility that it might have been the husband, Mike, and the possibility that it might have been any permutation of all the members of the family. But in the end, I felt it had to be Paula's story. I felt the wife and mother was in the best position to tell the story. But this feeling really came simultaneously with the feeling that she would be telling the story at this critical point of the night before an important revelation. Placing the narrative at that point was crucial. The two things arrived together and merged in the image of Paula lying awake while her husband, amazingly, is fast asleep. The novel really began for me with that image—as, in fact, it begins on the page. Mike, the husband, is the one who's going to have to do the talking anyway. He's going to have to do the actual telling, brief though it may be—brief but important—tomorrow. Paula is now, in advance of that, engaged in a whole other operation of telling, which puts the telling her husband will do in its fullest context. There are so many ways in which Paula does in fact speak not just for herself but for Mike and for her children. I can't now conceive of the novel as being narrated by anyone other than her. I wasn't impelled by the experiment of having a female narrator. I just felt she was right.

Q: And you didn't feel that crossing gender boundaries in your choice of narrator posed any extra challenges for you as a male writer?
A: Not a lot, no. Honestly, that was not important. Once I felt I knew her in the way that a novelist can feel they know a character, writing it as a female narrative—if that's even the right expression—was not a particular issue at all.

Q: You said that at one point you considered dividing the narrating burdens between not just Paula and Mike but also the twins. That would have involved exploring the impact which the announcement would have had on the twins, I suppose—otherwise they wouldn't have had much to say.
A: Exactly.

Q: This would have required you to carry the narrative beyond the point where, in the novel as we know it, Paula's voice goes silent, which is before anyone else wakes up and so before the crisis—if there is to be one—gets a chance to explode. This also strikes me as an innovation with respect to your earlier work, in which the starting point of the story is often a crisis situation in the narrative present that brings back the ghosts of the past, which the characters thought had been laid to rest. However, in *Tomorrow*

this moment of crisis is not recounted: it is anticipated with anxiety by Paula, but the novel comes to an end before it actually happens.
A: Yes, it's very much a novel about anticipation.

Q: Why is this so? Is it just the way it happened?
A: Well, the short answer would be precisely that. It's not a dishonest answer, it's a perfectly sincere answer. But if I'd included the twins in the narrative, that could not have been done, as you rightly say, except by pitching it all forward to some point in the future where this critical day would have happened. The children would have been told what Mike has to tell them, so they would then be able to express their thoughts and tell their story in the light of that event. And that would have then begged all kinds of questions. Where do you pitch it in the future? Is it going to be the day after, is it going to be years after? The repercussions of such a moment might be ones that would continue to affect the rest of the lives of those children. So where would you place it? Apart from that problem, it would anyway diffuse the intrinsic drama and tension of putting it right on the brink—literally on the eve—of this critical day. So I fairly quickly ruled out that the children were going to have any sort of voice. You have a novel which ends on the brink. No one knows, I don't know, what actually happens tomorrow. And that's just as I wanted it to be. A certain kind of reader, I can see, might say, "You've deprived me of the outcome, I don't know what the ending is." I can only say, "Well, that's one of the points." One of the curious things that any novelist or any storyteller has to deal with is the notion of an ending: how do things end? The fact is, in life there are no endings, apart from the obvious one. But in stories and fiction, there are endings: they are fabricated things. I try to be as honest and as responsive as I can be to the fact that in life there are no endings by writing the kind of novels—*Tomorrow* is perhaps the best example—where, in one sense, there is no ending, the ending is yet to come, and that ending anyway would be not so much an ending as a beginning, since it might have any number of different outcomes that could last a long time. That seems to me to reflect the way life is. Several of my novels end with an unknown outcome, with no real ending. *Waterland* does, *The Light of Day* does. Both *Out of This World* and *Last Orders* end in the air. If you write a novel which has a clear-cut ending, then you may be satisfying a certain kind of reader, but you are cheating on the way life really is. I want to write the kind of novels which become more mysterious at the end than they were at the beginning.

Q: *Tomorrow* has received some rather unfavorable reviews. Quite a few critics were disappointed with what they saw as the banality of the secret whose revelation the novel works toward, and which Paula fears might destroy her family. It concerns the twins' conception through artificial insemination, using an anonymous donor's sperm. The narrative hangs on the device of an explosive secret about to be disclosed, but some reviewers saw this secret as a huge letdown, not really worth all the fuss. After all, artificial insemination was hardly a shocking concept anymore in 1995, the year in which the novel is set. Is this a fair criticism, in your opinion?

A: I think it's thoughtless. There are two things here. One is the mechanistic notion of the novel just hanging upon a revelation, which supposedly keeps the reader guessing—that that's really what the novel is all about. To be honest, what I feel is that any intelligent, imaginative reader will probably guess what this revelation is quite quickly, possibly in the first pages of the novel. In any case, if they don't actually guess it, by the time it does get revealed—roughly halfway through—they will, I hope, have realized that the novel is about much more than merely waiting for this revelation. If it had just been about that, then I would have left the revelation to the end. But this is a minor point. The bigger thing is the nature of the revelation itself. There's a kind of reader, perhaps, who feels that any revelation must be outlandish, totally surprising, unguessable, because otherwise it's not worth it. I think, in fact, that the more commonplace, the less remote a revelation is—the more likely it could relate to any one of us—then the more meaningful it becomes. The revelation in *Tomorrow* is, indeed, nothing unusual, something that a lot of parents, families, children face. That's why the novel was worth writing. "What's the big deal?" it might be said, but it's a big deal in the sense that it's faced by a lot of people, and it can significantly affect their lives. It's one of those many things in life of which it's possible to say in the abstract, "What's the big deal?" That's because it's not happening to you. As soon as it happens to you, then you understand that the "not a big deal" is really a big deal after all. This is one of those essential things I think the novel is about, another article of faith. The business of imagining what it's like to be somebody else is also the business of saying to yourself, "Suppose this were happening to me." If you actually go along with that, empathetically, if you really think about what it would be like to be either a parent or a child who is on the giving or the receiving end of this bit of news, you very quickly realize that it's something that raises fundamental questions and can have enormous implications. It's core stuff. I think some critics of the novel simply haven't gone there.

Q: I find that an interesting way of looking at the allegedly anticlimactic structure of the novel. By generating suspense about the nature of the announcement, you're actually defamiliarizing it, inviting the reader to appreciate and learn anew how extraordinary such situations or moments really are and remain. While it's true that the situation in which Paula and Mike find themselves is hardly unique these days, and that the impact of the announcement they are planning to make the next morning may not be as devastating as she imagines, the point your novel is making is that, in spite of all this, it would be wrong simply to dismiss it as ordinary or mundane.

A: Absolutely. And even if we suppose that what occurs tomorrow is not devastating and that this family, which—although it is not all it seems—is actually a successful and loving family, carries on being that tomorrow and the day after tomorrow, as is not unlikely, there are still things out there on the edge of what seems to be the main issue which are very tricky indeed. One of the parts of that book which I found particularly engrossing is where the reflections on birth mingle inescapably with reflections on death—the thoughts that Paula has about what it will be like when either she or Mike is no longer there. If she goes first, then Mike will be able to see in the children a vestige of her, because she is the genuine mother. If it's the other way round and Mike goes first, then she won't be able to see any remnant of the husband she loves in the children. As soon as you start to go into that area where the facts of birth mingle with the facts of death, it gets very complicated.

Q: So the announcement does in fact have far-reaching consequences, even though on the face of it things may go on as normal.

A: Absolutely.

Q: An important theme of *Tomorrow* is the nature of the connections between parents and children. The novel seems to suggest that there can be different kinds of "family," that a family is not just blood relations or something that you are born into but can also be a voluntary association. In fact, questions of kinship have always been central to your work, which features a considerable number of substitute father figures and children who are adopted or whose paternity is uncertain or in dispute. For example, in *Waterland*, there is Mary Metcalf's aborted baby, who may or may not be Tom Crick's son; Dick Crick, the product of an incestuous union between Helen Atkinson and her father, who is adopted by Helen's husband Henry; and Tom's star pupil Price, whom he at one point refers to as "my son." In *Shuttlecock*, Prentis junior finds a father substitute in his boss. *Ever After*'s

Bill Unwin is adopted by his "Uncle" Sam after losing his father, who turns out not to have been his biological father after all. In *Last Orders*, we have Vince, a war baby adopted by Jack and Amy, who also find surrogate daughters in Mandy and Sally. And now in *Tomorrow*, there is the question of the twins' paternity, but also of Mike's multiple fathers (his "real" father, Grandpa Pete; his Uncle Eddie; his honorary "Uncle" Tim). How do you explain your constant concern with the nature of kinship relations?

A: Well, I would say that kinship, family relationships, family bonds, whether we like it or not, raise for us the big questions: where do we come from, and where are we going? How is it that I am here and I am the person I am, and will there be anything left of me when I'm gone? Factors of kinship also raise the big question of whether we are governed by biological forces, by nature, or by the human bonds we form. What you have in *Tomorrow* is the irony of a family which is in one sense not quite real, which is semi-artificial, but in another sense, emotionally, all the bonds seem to be there and seem to be more effective and more binding than they can be in a lot of families where the biological connection is a hundred percent. But in any case, I think when you write about families, you inevitably touch on those core human areas of origins and destiny. I found, curiously, when I went back to *Waterland*, some remarkable similarities between that novel and *Tomorrow*. They're both concerned with birth, and misbirth, in one form or another. They both address children. Paula isn't literally speaking to her children, of course: she's addressing her children in some strange chamber of her mind—and that's exactly what Tom Crick is doing. He uses the word "children" about his former students. He's speaking to a kind of class in his head. But both Tom and Paula have in common a concern for how the past translates into the future. In *Waterland*, you have the whole issue—excuse the pun—of the abortion, the child that never was, the child whose ghost, as it were, comes back in the form of a snatched baby. The power of biology. The stuff of birth.

Q: Still, I'm struck by the upbeat tone of *Tomorrow* and the contrast this presents to the much more muted tone of *Waterland*, or indeed most of your earlier work. While there was already a fair amount of optimism in *Last Orders* and especially *The Light of Day*, this is the closest you have ever come to writing about sheer happiness, about people leading basically contented and fulfilled lives—a fiendishly difficult subject for a novel, it seems to me.

A: Yes, happiness isn't a narrative, it's a state.

Q: I find it hard to see, therefore, how you could go down this road any further—so in a sense I'm not so surprised that you're taking a break from fiction and turning to nonfiction at this point in your career.

A: When I give readings from *Tomorrow*, I sometimes introduce them by mentioning the famous beginning from *Anna Karenina*: "All happy families are alike; every unhappy family is unhappy in its own way." I'd dispute Tolstoy's sweeping generalization—though this was hardly a motive in writing my book. What Tolstoy is implying is, "Let's forget about those happy families, who are boring and uninteresting, and let's deal with the unhappy families, where there is drama and excitement"—which is simply unfair. I think I wanted to say that happiness has its place in fiction and can even have its drama. *Tomorrow* is driven by the joy of possession brought up against the fear of loss. And I don't feel it's left me with nowhere to go; I don't feel it's the end of a road.

Q: I'd like to hear more about your reaction to the critical reception of your work. On the whole, your work is held in very high regard by critics, but when it is criticized, the reasons why often contradict each other. For example, while some find your work overly intellectual, cerebral, schematic, not from the heart, others find it overly emotional, sentimental, even melodramatic. What do you make of these conflicting appreciations? How do you account for them, and which one do you agree with least?

A: Well, I'm not sure I need to account for them. Critics are these people who speak their minds about your books. There's nothing I can do or should do about it. I try not to trouble myself too much about the opinions of critics and reviewers. It becomes easier not to be troubled, the more you write. I'm of course simply human, like any writer: it's nice to get a nice review, it's not nice to get a hostile review. But you framed your question within the polarization of the intellectual and the emotional. I think, generally speaking, critics like to be intellectual. They feel themselves to be intellectual figures, often to the extent that they can be wary of emotions.

Q: Do you feel that the intellectual element of your work has been overemphasized by critics, at the expense of the emotional dimension?

A: It may work in that direction. I think often the emotional content of my work may have been skirted by critics who find it hard, as I've just suggested, to write about emotion. It's not easy, actually, to write about emotion in five hundred words. Nonetheless, it should happen if a work has emotional content. Ordinary readers can get as emotional as they like in the invisible, private act of reading. God knows, you can cry over a book. No critic particularly wants to say, "I cried" or "I got emotional." It's embarrassing to do that in public. I hope that as a writer I embrace both things—the emotional and the intellectual. I want to be a writer who produces narratives which touch the heart, which move the reader, which generate emotion, and in some ways I want to do that more, maybe, than the other thing, of provoking thought. But I hope that both dimensions are there. You can't really have one without the other.

Q: Are there any other aspects of your work that you feel have been largely overlooked by critics and that you wish would receive more attention?
A: I have been sometimes thought of as gloomy or pessimistic, but I think my work is far from being all darkness. We've been talking about the happiness in *Tomorrow*, and the book before that was called *The Light of Day*. It contains some dark things, it's about a murder, but it doesn't have its title for nothing. It contains a lot of light. I think there's a lot of humor in my work, even quite a lot of comedy. I'm sometimes tempted to describe *Last Orders* as a comic novel, which might surprise some people. Perhaps what I'm saying is that the light and dark go together; you have to do both. I believe, in any case, that whatever the subject matter, fiction is an inherently positive thing. I like to use the word "creative," a word which has become—I don't quite know why—rather unfashionable, but I think what I do is a creative thing, and I think being creative is positive. The mere business—or the not-so-mere business—of starting from nothing and creating the whole world that a novel can be is inherently positive, the business of bringing things to life. I think that fiction is always at some level celebratory. Even when it's exploring some of the most dismal aspects of experience, it's doing that, it's not being inert. And doesn't any novel simply want to offer, whatever else it may be doing, the stuff, the flavor, the taste of life? Isn't it constantly reminding you of the feeling of being in this world, and urging you not to be complacent or indifferent about it? "No, look again at that tree, have a look at that tree that you haven't noticed, just think for a moment, isn't that a wonderful tree?" I think that fiction should be constantly having such little—or not-so-little—effects. They may be almost subliminal, or they may be the point of a whole paragraph, but they're saying, "This is life, this is what we have, look at it!" Isn't that inherently celebratory? As you get older, the more precious things become, not less. It's as simple as that. The more of your life that you've lived, the less of your life that you have yet to live, the more you value the stuff that's there. If you're a writer, the more, perhaps,

your work will want to reflect, before you go, what can be good about this often terrible world we live in. One doesn't have to think very far, or need to have lived that long, to know that it can be a terrible world. But it can be also very good. It's very good that we're sitting here right now, able to talk like this.

Graham Swift's *Making an Elephant*

Ramona Koval / 2009

From *The Book Show. Radio National Programs.* http://www.abc.net.au/radionational /programs/archived/bookshow/graham-swifts-making-an-elephant/3059886. Reprinted by permission of ABC Library Sales.

British author Graham Swift talks about his new collection of non-fiction stories and poetry *Making An Elephant*. It is in many ways about how Swift came to be a writer, and about the mentors, friends and experiences he's had along the way.

Ramona Koval: I've interviewed Graham Swift before, it was at the Edinburgh International Book Festival on the publication of his novel *Tomorrow*. He is immensely polite and informative, but you'd have to say he's self-effacing, maybe even a little guarded. But in his new book, which is not a novel but a collection of non-fiction pieces he's written over the years, he lets us into the mind of Graham Swift the writer in a way that his novels don't. It's called *Making an Elephant: Writing from Within* and it's in many ways about how he came to be a writer, what being a writer means to the way you live, and it's about the mentors, friends and experiences he's had along the way. Graham Swift's books *Waterland* and *Last Orders* were both made into films, and *Last Orders* won the 1996 Booker Prize, you might remember, and there are in this book, his thoughts on films and prizes as well. Graham joins us from our ABC London studios. Welcome to *The Book Show*, Graham.
Graham Swift: Hello.

Ramona Koval: You say that you have a photo of Isaac Babel on your work desk. Tell me why, of all the writers you could have chosen it was Isaac Babel, the Russian writer, it was he who took pride of place?

Graham Swift: Well, I'd have to take you back to when I was pretty young. I was still in my teens, I was seventeen, I think turning eighteen, I'd just left school, I had a place at university and like a lot of people in that situation then I took myself off with a rucksack on my back to travel very roughly, in my case around the eastern Mediterranean, Greece, Turkey, parts of the Middle East. And at that time I think the desire, the ambition to be a writer was pretty firmly implanted in me, but I hadn't done much about it in practical terms. Looking back, I honestly think this was because I was, in a way, as afraid of my ambition and the demands it might make of me as I was obviously gripped by it, and it was also a very solitary ambition. I didn't come from a background . . . from a family which had any writers in it, I had no one to push me in the direction of being a writer, no mentor figure, with the exception of a few other writers who I would meet, as it were, by reading them.

One particular writer who you mentioned, Isaac Babel, a Russian writer who I could never have met literally because he died, like a lot of writers, in mysterious circumstances under Stalin in the '40s. But I met him, as it were, in this very significant way in, of all places, Greece when I was coming to the end of this period of travelling in which in fact I'd hardly read a book. It was a very unliterary few months in fact. But just before I was due to get a train all the way back to London, I had a bit of time on my hands and amazingly some money left and I thought I should read a book. And I went into this bookshop in Greece, I found an English language section, and from it ironically I picked out the stories by this Russian writer, in translation of course. It was a Penguin edition . . .

Ramona Koval: Was that *Red Cavalry*?
Graham Swift: It's called *Red Cavalry*, I still have this book. What can I say? I sat down in the warm Greek sunshine and I was completely electrified by what I read. I think this happens really very rarely that you meet, as I put it, another writer through their work. You don't always get totally ignited by what you read, and nor do you feel, as I felt with Babel, that I had, as it were, made a friend. I felt that if I could have met him in real life we would have got on, we would have been able to talk into the night and so on. And as I found out more about Babel, what really inspired me was that I discovered that he himself was the kind of writer who didn't think he was a natural writer, he always thought he was very writerly, rather intellectual. He struggled with his writing, but to this wonderful effect.

I, at that time, as I say, seventeen, eighteen, I thought I wasn't a natural writer. After all, if I was a natural writer I'd already have become a more fully fledged writer. I thought that in order to become a writer I would have to make myself one, I would have to work very hard at it. And I was rather scared of all of that work. So there was a rapport with Babel in that sense too and, as I say in *Making an Elephant*, I've now come to believe that the idea of the natural writer is possibly a rather bogus one. The natural writers are the ones like in fact Babel who make it seem natural, but all writers really have to work.

Ramona Koval: But Babel had, I suppose, a natural subject didn't he because he was in such a moment of history and was part of the red cavalry and he had things to report on, he had pogroms and battles and characters.
Graham Swift: Yes, he was in this extraordinary position, he was this pretty intellectual, bespectacled, Jewish intellectual from Odessa who, during the post-revolutionary wars, found himself attached to a regiment of Cossack cavalry, and thus you would think entirely out of his depth, an extraordinary clash of different worlds. But out of this period when he rode with these red cavalry came these extraordinary stories, really very intense, very physical, violent, but lyrical at the same time.

Ramona Koval: Do you think it was reportage or. . . ?
Graham Swift: I think it went beyond that. No, I don't think reportage would be a good description. I mean, you could say that had he not had that experience the stories could never have happened, but I think they are real literature, they are great writing.

Ramona Koval: I'm asking that because you say in the book that 'the average adult is embarrassed by things made up,' and the idea of a grown man sitting in his study making stuff up . . . is that what you mean about the embarrassment of fiction?
Graham Swift: Yes, I remember writing that phrase. I would stick by it. I've been a writer for . . . I hate to think, it's decades now, and I constantly come across and, I have to say, get rather baffled by and sometimes rather wearied by this notion of fiction of something that must be autobiographical. You get the question, 'What was it that happened to you that made you write this novel? What was it in your experience that caused this novel to be?' And when I say, 'Well, actually, nothing really because I made this thing up, I created it, I caused it to be,' then that gets a rather baffled response from my questioner.

I think people, even some readers who quite habitually read fiction, do have this stubborn view that it must be in some way fact that has been turned into fiction. And for me the great joy and challenge and glory of fiction is that it is creative, which is a rather unfashionable word these days, but I think it is the creative element of fiction, the making something come into being and come alive that simply wasn't there before, which gives it its real excitement and the kind of excitement which will galvanise the reader, whereas merely to turn fact into fiction seems to me . . . I mean, it's obviously something that can produce some great results but it seems to me to be a rather limited, unexciting kind of adventure.

Ramona Koval: That title, *Making an Elephant*, is from a piece where you remember your father who was a civil servant in London but before that had been a pilot in WWII, and as a child you made him a wooden elephant. Tell me about that story.

Graham Swift: Well, that's the explanation of the rather mysterious title of this book. The title of the book, as you say, is the title of one of the central pieces in the book, and it is essentially a piece about my dad who was for most of his life a civil servant who sat at a desk more of his time, but who had been, obviously before I was around, a pilot in the navy, a fighter pilot, and naval fighter pilots had a particularly heroic task as they had to land on these ridiculous swaying surfaces of aircraft carriers.

My dad had these two lives; he had a life in the war and he had a life as I knew him, which was very conventional. He died over fifteen years ago now, and I certainly still miss him. He was a very practical man, to a pitch where you might have thought he was not particularly imaginative, although I think you would have been wrong. But he was absolutely in his element doing jobs around the house, any kind of handiwork, making things with wood, anything to do with machines, car engines and so on, all the things, in other words, which as a head-in-the-clouds novelist I've been pretty hopeless at myself.

But there was this one moment when I was actually quite a small boy when for whatever reason I made an attempt to pay a little tribute to my dad's handyman skills and I made this wooden elephant, didn't make such a bad job of it, it was actually quite a simple task in some ways. But this episode has a little twist to it which, as I look back from quite a long time now of being a writer, it just seemed to me to encapsulate a lot of things about my relationship with my father and, in a way, to turn around a kind of standard perception I had of it.

It was a moment when he became the fantasist, the imaginative person and I oddly became the realist because it was all to do with painting this elephant, and he wanted me to paint it pink or yellow, and I thought this was a crazy idea, elephants were grey. I insisted on painting it grey, and as I looked back now I wish I had painted it pink.

Ramona Koval: But if you decided against grey you might have had a different life and maybe not been a writer at all.

Graham Swift: Possible. I think a lot was actually contained in this little episode because, after all, fiction writers have to be both very imaginative people but they have to marry that to the real world. One of the essences of the novel as a form is that it brings together the imagination and realism in an extraordinary way. I suppose at that point when I was a boy . . . and even then, I'm talking about when I was seven or eight, I think I was nursing the desire to be a writer. Even then I had this part of me that was nonetheless a realist and wanted to be honest about how things really were.

Ramona Koval: The way you describe it, in a sense you were kind of meeting each other halfway. You were offering the elephant and he was saying to you "I'll offer the creativity and you paint it pink or yellow and so something other than grey that you might have expected me to like."

Graham Swift: I think you're right, there was a sort of crossover going on because, after all, my dad then . . . I was making a toy elephant and I think my dad was rather pleased by the fact that I was doing something so out of character, but in a way he might have been going back to his childhood and to the world of toys when elephants could be pink or yellow, and I, on the other hand, as the boy was in a way being grown up, perhaps rather boringly grown up by insisting on the greyness.

Ramona Koval: But you insisted on the elephantness of it.

Graham Swift: Yes, indeed. I related it to the real world of real elephants that are always grey. Another little twist to the story is that when my dad was a pilot in the war, ironically he had a period when he was based on land in Africa in Kenya. So he would have flown around Mt. Kilimanjaro, around there, and undoubtedly would have seen from the air those herds of animals, including real elephants. That was a memory he'd never shared with me but in that piece I imagined myself as him looking down from his cockpit and seeing real grey elephants.

Ramona Koval: I should ask what happened to the elephant?
Graham Swift: I still have it as a permanent reminder of everything we've been talking about. It's quite a precious object now.

Ramona Koval: So when you talk about the beginnings of your writerly life, you talk about the relationship with a particular editor and a mentor, and you talk about having fifty-nine rejection slips for one piece . . .
Graham Swift: I don't remember the number fifty-nine but quite a lot of rejection slips, whatever the actual number was . . .

Ramona Koval: Oh I know what it is, it's on page fifty-nine. I've written "'59, rejection slips."
Graham Swift: Well, you might well be close, let's call it fifty-nine.

Ramona Koval: However many rejection slips, how did you manage to get over that?
Graham Swift: Well, just by determination, by sometimes rather grim determination and a sort of faith. As I said, I had no-one to assist me, to be my guide in becoming a writer, it was absolutely down to me, and for a very long time this meant I was just kind of out in the cold, teaching myself to write, being an apprentice writer. I started to have some links with some magazines of that time, I'm talking about the '70s really, and I would send off short stories to magazines, and at that time I hadn't written a novel, it was only stories.

And I formed gradually a particular link with a magazine called *London* magazine which was run and edited by this wonderful man called Alan Ross, who's sadly not around anymore. But I started to have a sort of tenuous relationship with him because I would send him stories and invariably he'd send back a rejection slip, but on the rejection slip he would in his own handwriting just put some little note, some little message which gave me hope and made me think that he actually cared. Each rejection slip seemed to bring me closer and closer to the point where I wouldn't be rejected, I'd be accepted, and that finally came and it was a marvellous moment.

Ramona Koval: Because I should just say, those words that he'd write were, you say, "sorry" or "almost" or "not quite" or "very nearly."
Graham Swift: This may sound a little pathetic to people who have never been in such a situation, but those "almosts" and "not quites" meant a very

great deal to me. And when he finally did publish a first story of mine, then there were others, and I got to meet him. I knew that I hadn't been wrong. My instinct was that I had a friend or a friend of my writing, as Alan was, and he was really the first person of his kind that I'd ever met. He was a writer himself, he was a poet, he was an editor and publisher, he moved in the world of literary and artistic things, and I had simply never met someone like that. So he was the person who, as it were, said to me "come in from the cold," he opened a door.

Ramona Koval: And he opened a door holding a drink, didn't he.

Graham Swift: Yes. In fact the piece I have written about him is a tribute not just to him but to Alan's favourite drink which was this thing called the Negroni, which was a kind of mixture of Campari, red vermouth, gin and various other things. When I first met him he took me out to lunch and I'd never been taken out to lunch in such a way, somewhere in Chelsea, and he said, "What do you want to drink? I'm going to have a Negroni, what would you like?" Of course I'd never heard of a Negroni, didn't know what the hell it was, but of course I said yes, I'd love one. And it was a lovely drink, went very quickly to my head, which wasn't difficult because the whole situation was going to my head, and I've always associated that drink with Alan. I subsequently found out that many other writers who Alan nursed and brought on (and there were many now quite well-known names that he first published) had a similar experience. They were offered a Negroni. So it's a drink that's always been rather special for me.

Ramona Koval: He was also a man who suffered from depression and he would disappear, you say, for some time and the he would resurface, you say, "looking fragile but very pleased to be back in the world and generally playing down the whole thing." And then you say "writers should count themselves lucky merely to have their self-induced immurements, their self-imposed immersions."

Graham Swift: Yes, that's a piece which rather takes up the feeling that you can of course get, as a writer, that you're kind of immured and writing is this thing that you have to sit alone in a room and do, and sometimes it can feel like a bit of a prison. And particularly when you're a struggling writer who has never quite broken into print, you feel you're never going to get out of this sealed chamber. I really do think that if you're going to be a writer you have to be able to live with this, you have to be able to be alone with yourself and sometimes come up against yourself in some quite challenging ways, all of which can be tough but nothing like as tough as the claustrophobia that Alan suffered from.

He had these bouts of depression. They would entail going away somewhere and being, in a sense, locked up and getting medication and so on. And in Alan's case this actually stemmed from a wartime experience of his. There is a link, oddly with my father. Alan was in the navy and he had a ghastly experience of being in a ship that was under fire and being trapped between bulkheads in a ship in a very nasty predicament and he may never have got out, although obviously he did. And I think this was one possible cause of his depression, and it oddly caught up with him much later in his life. I don't know if you can remember the Russian submarine called the *Kursk* . . .

Ramona Koval: Yes, that's right, and all those young men being trapped.
Graham Swift: It went to the bottom with all those sailors trapped in it, and this I know was very haunting for Alan, partly because he'd been, like in fact my father, on convoys to Russia, to Murmansk, and I think the *Kursk* went down quite near Murmansk. So such really terrible experiences far exceed the trials of an author sitting alone in a room, but there is that claustrophobic connection.

Ramona Koval: Let's imagine you in this room and you're writing your novels, and then you say that between novels, to keep your engine running you write poetry. I want you to read one of your poems and then I want to talk to you about them. Can you read "The Bookmark" for me?
Graham Swift: Yes, since we're on a book show, I think it would be a good one to read.
[*Reading from* "All the books you . . ." *to* ". . . it must have been you."]

Ramona Koval: Lovely. That's "The Bookmark" by Graham Swift, and you actually have a picture of a bus ticket in the book.
Graham Swift: Yes, one of the pleasures of doing this book is that it gave me an opportunity that I've never had before to include some illustrations, photographs and so on, to go with the pieces. So yes, with the poems there is . . . the bookmark, a London transport bus ticket of some era quite long in the past.

Ramona Koval: Yes, and it reminds me of a Melbourne tram ticket of some era long in the past, and I was looking at it the other day and I was thinking look at all these numbers on it, it's got number one to twenty-six, and I thought what were they, that's not the days of the month . . .

Graham Swift: I think those numbers on the London transport ticket are the fare stages. That is to say, they are the stops on the bus route. So the conductor would clip the ticket to indicate the journey on the right number, the right fare to go with it. That's my theory anyway.

Ramona Koval: It sounds plausible to me. I was going to mention this at the end but while we're talking about illustrations, at the very, very end of this book, just next to the endpaper, there's a beautiful illustration of . . . are they flies? Are they for trout fishing or salmon fishing?

Graham Swift: They are salmon flies, in fact.

Ramona Koval: That's how much about fishing I know, but they are gorgeous, and then I just looked a bit closer and it's got "GS 1994."

Graham Swift: Yes, I have to confess they are salmon flies which I tied myself. Fishing is one of the things I do when I'm not writing, and in my time I've caught some salmon, not very many, they're quite hard to catch or I find them hard to catch. But I tied some flies of my own, and there is a particular thrill to catch a fish on a fly that you have tied yourself.

Ramona Koval: So this looks like it's got feathers or something.

Graham Swift: Yes, all kinds of lovely materials; feathers, bits of gold wire, silver wire, bits of silk, and there are hundreds of patterns, as they're called, for different flies. I didn't entirely invent this one . . .

Ramona Koval: This is called "Thunder and Lightning."

Graham Swift: Yes, "Thunder and Lightning," it has a lot of orange in it, in fact, which you can't see in the illustration.

Ramona Koval: But I imagine they would take a long time, a very patient time.

Graham Swift: Yes, you do need a bit of patience but, like many things, you get into a rhythm with it, you start to not have to refer to the book, as it were, you just do it.

Ramona Koval: And where does fishing come in your writing life?

Graham Swift: It sort of rather comes in and out of my writing life. It's something that I've always had a yen for. I fished as a boy, and I effectively gave it up for a while when writing started to predominate in my life, but there was a time around . . . *Waterland* came out in the mid, early 1980s, and I happened to meet a new very good friend who was a great fisherman and who took me fishing again and specifically fly fishing. He taught me how to cast and how to sometimes catch trout and rarely salmon. So I came back to it at that point in my life, and oddly there was a further marvellous coincidence because I did quite a lot of my fishing down in north Devon where Ted Hughes lived, and I actually met him via some mutual friends and I met him through fishing rather than through writing, or poetry in his case. I had some good times with Ted which were really all to do with being by or indeed in rivers. The book I think generally pays tribute to some writer friends I've had and have, and to the strange ways in which you meet them which aren't necessarily to do with literary matters at all.

Ramona Koval: What about that little gift that Ted Hughes gave you on the bank?

Graham Swift: That's another thing which I wish . . . I mean, I said I've still got that wooden elephant, this is something I wish I still had. I was once fishing with Ted in Devon and it was one of those rare days when I caught and unfortunately lost a salmon, quite a sizable one . . .

Ramona Koval: Oh yes, this is the fishing story! "It was huge!"

Graham Swift: I have to say that. And I had a consolation prize because I did actually catch and land another salmon which wasn't as big. But more importantly when that second salmon was being landed on the bank, Ted . . . he noticed something, there was a sort of shingle bank, this was a river in Devon, and he picked up this object and I saw that it was a little skull. Ted said, "This is a pike's skull and I think you should have it."

That was a marvellous moment, you couldn't have made it up because there was a time in my life when I only knew Ted, I had only met Ted through his poetry and I'm going back to when I was a schoolboy and I read those wonderful early books of poems of his, including that very famous poem called "*Pike*," which is one of his most well-known poems. There I was, much later in life, with the man himself, actually fishing with him, and what happens? He picks up a pike's skull and says, "Here you are, you should have it as a souvenir."

Ramona Koval: How did you lose it? My goodness me!

Graham Swift: I'm coming to the sad part of the story which is that I lost it, and I lost it in the way that fishermen can lose things, not just fish. They take around with them all this paraphernalia of tackle and throw it in the back of a car, and it all gets jumbled up and you lose some of these bits and pieces, and foolishly and to my eternal regret I must have somehow put this pike skull somewhere where it got jumbled up with something I threw away.

Ramona Koval: We've all done that Graham, don't worry.
Graham Swift: Anyway, it was gone. So the loss . . .

Ramona Koval: But it lives in your writing.
Graham Swift: The loss of that pike skull was of course far more important than the loss of that salmon.

Ramona Koval: Yes. The whole idea of fishing reminds me of some of your writing where things are going on underneath to great depth from something that looks sort of smooth and regular and familiar.
Graham Swift: I think that fishing is one of the activities . . . I mean, you can stretch it a bit too far, but it's one of those activities which you can compare to writing, it has analogies with writing. Ted Hughes himself wrote about this, and I think it's really all to do with your dealing with a surface, the surface of water and you don't know what is there underneath. Sometimes you can see what's there but a lot of the time you can't, and a lot of the time there's nothing there, and then you may get taken by a huge surprise. I think that's not unlike the creative process of writing. No day is like the last day or the next, you don't know what's going to be there, if anything, beneath the surface. But you're constantly trying to make a connection with something that is lying perhaps mysteriously waiting for you.

Ramona Koval: Well, there's a lot more in the book that's lying mysteriously waiting for the readers because we haven't even skimmed the surface of the depths of the book. The book is called *Making an Elephant: Writing from Within*, and it's published in Australia by Picador. Graham Swift, thank you so much for being on *The Book Show*.
Graham Swift: Thank you very much, it's been a pleasure.

Graham Swift Unpacks His Archive

Jamie Andrews / 2009

From a Guardian Books podcast interview, http://www.bl.uk/podcasts/podcast92584.html, conducted at the British Library. Reprinted by courtesy of the British Library Board.

The British Library has acquired the archive of the Booker Prize winning novelist Graham Swift. It includes handwritten manuscripts and drafts of his eight acclaimed novels. It also includes correspondence with friends and contemporaries and includes exchanges with his cherished angling companion, the late Ted Hughes, and his English teacher at Dulwich College in the 1960s. Jamie Andrews from British Libraries spoke to Graham Swift about the archive.

JA: So Graham, welcome to the British Library.
GS: Thank you. And perhaps I should thank everyone who's made all this possible myself.

JA: We're going to start by talking about your archive. My first question is, when did you start to think of your papers as an archive as such, as opposed to a collection of file boxes that were maybe cluttering or clogging up your study or your attic?
GS: Well, it's obviously something which comes with age. I mean when I set out to be a writer, I think the idea that my manuscripts and so on would become an archive would have been quite dreamlike. The fact is that as you write more and more, you build up all this stuff, and, of course you have a decision on whether to keep it or not, and I have to say that I have thrown away stuff. I have sometimes thrown away stuff in a really quite aggressive way because I didn't like what I had written. But most of it I've kept; and it just seems that there comes a point where a kind of critical mass builds up, and you say to yourself, "Well, what am I going to do with all this stuff?" And I could keep it but the sheer volume of it starts to become a problem.

So I guess I started to think of it as an archive maybe five or six years ago, and now officially as well.

JA: When the archive as such was in your home, how often did you go back to old material? And how actively did you sort or arrange it?

GS: I think there were long periods where it simply gathered dust, and, to be specific, most of it went up into my loft, and I don't go up into the loft very often myself. So there weren't that many occasions when I felt the urge to refer to things there. And obviously if I did they would have been fairly recent things. But I'd like to think that, as I stored things away, I did so in quite an orderly fashion. I just thought that if I am going to put this stuff out of sight, do it in a careful way, not just shove it in a box and leave it as a mess. So it is, I suppose, as archives go, I don't know you would know better than me, relatively orderly.

JA: That was my impression actually. It was more ordered than that, almost exceptionally orderly, and I noticed in your book *Making an Elephant* there's a memoir of your father where you talk about the way you would look into his photograph albums and how he carefully indexed and labelled them. Do you think that that kind of ordering is something that you got from him?

GS: It could be to some extent, although I'd have to say that there is part of me which is extremely messy, and indeed there is part of the writer in me which is extremely messy because writing itself, I think, is a very muddled, and messy, and mysterious, and sometimes confusing thing. If you were to look at any average page of my manuscripts, I think you would see that straight away they are extremely messy, quite indecipherable in some cases. I always have used pen and ink. I've always crossed out a great deal. There are lots of squiggles and lines and arrows, so, in that sense, I would say, I'm not at all organized.

JA: Hmm, ok, that's interesting. You mention that, of course, an archive draft follows twists and turns and false routes, do you ever get nostalgic for what might have been in a work, or a direction that a character or a narrative may have taken? And do you ever regret or have you regretted once you've had a novel published that actually you should have stuck with draft seven or six or something?

GS: Nothing quite as solid as that. Um, in fact, nowhere near that. Usually, by the time I've finished something, I'm satisfied that at that point it is finished. That's really it. I don't often revisit my work. Certainly don't sit down and reread it, like an old reader would. When I do that though I would, I think, sometimes look at a sentence and think "Oh, I wish I had written that sentence in a slightly different way, I'd be sort of satisfied, dissatisfied with it, in a kind of detailed sense, but as a whole, I'm usually, by the time I'm ready to part with it, quite sure that that is indeed the case. It can go out into the world now. So I haven't had big second thoughts about, you know, plot lines and characters then.

JA: And how are you sure, how do you know when you have arrived at that moment when it can go out into the world? How do you know you've finished?

GS: It's an instinctive thing. It's sort of an intuitive thing. It's partly also a process of sheer exhaustion. You feel there is nothing more I can do with it. I think all writers have, to some degree, a desire to be perfect, to write the perfect novel, but, of course, that's impossible, but you strive to get close to it. And, in fact, in practice, what happens is you say to yourself, "Well, this is the best I could do with this, and it's now ready to go."

JA: You're talking about this striving for perfection, do you ever find yourself in a condition to be reworking a sentence, or a phrase, over and over again to get to that perfect form?

GS: It can happen. I think it's entirely unpredictable. On any given day I could, on the one hand, spend hours working on effectively a paragraph, or indeed a sentence, and at the end of that day, even having done all that work, deciding it's not right. In another day, in the same space of hours, I could write several pages, and be happy with those pages. And I think that is, that is one of the frustrations of course, but it's also one of the excitements of writing: it is you never know what is going to happen. Generally speaking I'm certainly capable of revising a great deal. I do rewrite a great deal. It's rare, even if it is joyful when it happens, that it's right the first time but most of it is a hard slog.

JA: One thing that struck me, looking at your archive, was that there's an awful lot of paper and ink there. And not an awful lot of typewritten or word-processed, and that is becoming more and more rare with contemporary writers where a draft exists as a physical object. They may well be printed out with hundreds of emendations but none of them printed out, or they may not even exist as physical objects. They're related only to files on someone's hard drive or in the cloud. Have you ever been tempted to change your writing patterns, to take account of new technological advances in literary production? Or are you resolutely sticking with ink and paper?

GS: Well, yes, I think I am deep down, stubbornly, a pen-and-ink person. I'm not a total Luddite. I have got a computer. I was relatively late in moving to a computer. Before that I had various typewriters, but the actual real creative work, the kind of composition, I think just has to be done with pen and ink. I don't think there has been a case, ever, where I've sat down, as it were, the stage where you have a blank mind, and thought, "What am I going to write now?" and done that on the computer. I'd have to do that with a piece of paper. And I think the computer is a little bit, maybe not just a little bit, deluding, because when you see this lovely typeface coming up on the screen, it tempts you to think, "Oh, this is marvelous. It looks like a book already." And my rule is always, at least, print it out before you accept it. And I move to a computer in the last stages, last drafts, and, of course, it's wonderful at that point because in the old days with a typewriter all corrections had to be laboriously dealt with, and they are very quickly dealt with on a computer. So, for the final stages it's a real boon. It speeds things up, but I won't be getting rid of my fountain pen.

JA: A fountain specifically, a fountain pen?

GS: Ah, yeah, in fact I've written all my books with two fountain pens. One sort of packed up and one is still going. And that's always going to be the case.

JA: I find that very interesting because I can write notes on paper but I can't write anything substantial unless it's on the screen because I like to put random ideas up, out there, and then shape them. My sense has always been that if you write by hand, at least in the initial stage, you have to do a lot of writing in your head first before it comes down to the paper. Is that something you'd recognize?

GS: That may be the case, although I'm not really aware of it. What I do feel is that the pen gets stuff from your head onto the page amazingly quickly. And it does it in a way which means something to you. I mean when I'm writing at the manuscript stage, no one else is going to look at it. It's important that I understand it. So, in using a pen, I can not only put words down and, if I want to, rapidly cross them out and put alternatives and all that stuff, I can put all kinds of little squiggles and symbols in the margin, very rapidly with a pen, which will mean something to me. And my fear, at that stage, is always that I will lose something because my powers of mental retention don't get any better. My short term memory is not what it once was, and I'm always worried that I will lose something, whether it's something I need now, or whether, as is often the case, it's a little idea I have for something coming up. And I need to make a note of it very quickly, and I think the pen is a perfect instrument for that.

JA: Do you always carry a notebook around with you wherever you go?

GS: Oddly no. But I've always got some sort of piece of paper on me. I'm rather against the idea of walking around with a notebook on me that would make me feel too much like a kind of writer. [laughter] But I'm certainly often in the position, if an idea comes to me, I'm sitting on a tube train, or whatever, and I have to rapidly note it, and I'll get out some bit of paper in my wallet or whatever, and I hope I got a pen or a pencil and make a quick note of it. If I don't do that, I often find myself constructing little memory devices so that I won't let that thing go, whether it's a key word or not. That business of retaining the thing that you need to use is terribly important.

JA: Can you remember any unlikely place where the first idea or a crucial idea for one of your novels came to you?

GS: Oddly, I think I have to say no to that. It would be marvelous to have that memory clearly, if only because writers are often asked that very question by journalists, you know, "How did it happen? What was the first thing?" It would be nice to give them a clear answer. Unfortunately, it doesn't work like that. What happens, I think, is that, almost without knowing it, you are aware that you have something going, you have something on your hands, you've somehow crossed the line, and you're into something, even though you can't really say where that line was. My novels certainly don't begin with grand, big ideas. I think they begin with small things which grow. But they begin in a very confused way too. It's groping in the dark quite a lot.

JA: Back to the archive again. We've just been into the manuscript stacks, where all our manuscripts and archives are stored, because we wanted to show you where your papers are now going to be living. And they are living just facing the archive of Ted Hughes, which is a nice correspondence because I believe you were friends. You knew each other and you fished together . . .

GS: That's right.

JA: . . . for a while. How does it feel firstly, to see what up until recently was such familiar, almost banal file boxes etc., now in a place like this?

And how does it feel when you walk away from them knowing they are not coming home with you again?

GS: Well, um, since you mention Ted Hughes's archive, which is at the moment apparently physically close to where you've put mine, I can't help feeling very touched and moved by that because Ted is not with us anymore, and he should still be with us. He died far too young. And so there is that effect it has to see his stuff. Just on my own stuff, I realize this is a rather humbling thing. Of course when my archive, which was, I think, seventy plus boxes of stuff, was in my house, it looked like a lot of stuff. For me it was a lot of stuff. Of course, it represents a large portion of my life. It's big in terms of years. When you see it here in the British Library, among all the other stuff, it looks tiny. It looks totally dwarfed, and that is perhaps a not unhealthy, humbling effect to know that, delighted though I am, that the material is here, it's just one little collection among lots of big ones.

JA: Hmm, well, I suppose the idea is that it's the connection that it makes: the fact that in your archive there are letters from Ted Hughes. You feature in Ted Hughes's archives, I believe, in his fishing diaries, and you recount some of his fishing trips. And there must be other connections as well, but because we haven't started to catalogue his papers yet we're not yet aware of. So does it feel both perhaps humbling in terms of size, but also that it's connecting into new networks?

GS: Well, yes, I think that is a very good point, and that is one I haven't really, fully realized yet. That, again, when these boxes were in my house, they were, in a sense, entirely isolated. Although, of course, they contain a great many connections with other people, with other writers—the letters and so on. And now those connections can be followed through. So, so, yes, it's, it's something which I suppose you could say is all growing in that sense.

JA: That's it. I mean the collections are never stable. They're constantly re-evaluated as soon as the new collection comes in because it changes the perspective of everything else, which is why I think it is so fascinating. Um, now objects, I think, in your work, it seems to me are an important feature, and they carry meaning across generations. So, for example, the bottle of Coronation Ale, bottles that in the case of Coronation Ale in *Waterland* or the notebooks in *Ever After* or even there is a bus ticket that you mention in one of your, or you did mention, in one of your poems that you find by accident and that transplants you back to another time. How do you feel your objects, your archive will be used, seen in the future? What do you expect people to do with it?

GS: Well, um, this isn't something that I have thought about deeply, I'd have to say, and maybe I should think about it more. My first thought, I suppose, is that this material now becomes the object of scholarly research. That people now will come here when the archive is ready, from pretty well everywhere, if they wish to go through this stuff. It's another way in which it will extend its kind of scope and, in a way, its size. I'm quite ready for that. I'm quite happy about that because, if only because, I have had a lot of people ask about access to things, which, while all the stuff was in my house, I wouldn't be prepared to allow. But through an institution that can happen much more efficiently.

JA: Hmm, okay. Well, if we move on now to your new book, which is published on the sixth of March and is called *Making an Elephant*, and the first thing, I think, that surprised me looking through the contents was that there's a series of poems, which are published in here. You're not, I think it is fair to say generally known for being a poet. How did you decide to bring these to publication? And when you wrote them was there always the idea that they'd appear in print or was that something that you focused on later?

GS: Well, the poems are possibly a one-off, I mean there are several poems, but collectively they're one-off because I'm not a poet. I suppose there is a sense in which I believe that poetry isn't just a matter of verse, so there is poetry in prose, and if people felt there was an element of poetry in my novels that would quite please me. But I'm not a poet in the sense that having written these specific things, known as poems before, the poems in *Making an Elephant* all come from around a strange period between two novels. I finished the novel called *The Light of Day*, and I was, in a sense I was just resting, but also starting to look for my next novel, which wasn't arriving. And out of a feeling of wanting to do something which would keep me fresh in this interval, I started to write some poems. I can't say why it should have happened at this particular point. But certainly what did happen, is, once I'd written one poem, another one popped up and then another one. And so for a period of several weeks, maybe months, I seemed to be writing poem after poem. And I thought, "What am I going to do with this stuff? Is this just my own personal delectation? Is it perhaps worth publishing in some way?" I certainly never thought that I would actually put them into a specific slim volume of poetry. I feel that would have been, that would have been rather audacious of me. But when the idea for this book, *Making an*

Elephant, began to evolve, generally, I thought well this is an opportunity to publish some of these poems, by no means all. And so, there they are.

JA: Was the process of drafting a composition markedly different from that of your other work?
GS: Uh, for poetry?

JA: Yes.
GS: Well, certainly pen and ink again. And as much crossing out as with prose if not more. The great thing, of course, was it's fast. Writing a novel, not all the poems, but writing many of the poems, was an astonishing rapid process. At least the first draft. It would come in a flash, and it was a delight for me to have this quickness of composition. When, obviously, novels are such long, laborious tasks. And I enjoyed that, and I enjoyed the sort of hopping from one poem to another. And so, it served as a really refreshing exercise if nothing else. But I'd like to think that some of the poems have some real meat to them. That they are worthy of their place in the book.

JA: It's interesting. My sense was that some of the forms were familiar to me. In terms of your themes that emerged, the everyday and transcendence, and historical forces, and water, there is still quite a lot of water in there. And themes that can be seen in your wider work as well. Is that something you recognized while you were writing them? After?
GS: I think I recognize the sort of things you're mentioning afterwards, and certainly when I was thinking of which ones might go into the book or not. And one thing I certainly noticed is that a number of the poems could be called narrative poems. None are very long but there are some relatively long poems, which tell a story in one way or another. And it's often effectively the story of a whole life, a very condensed story of a whole life, a whole character evolving, which, of course, is not a million miles from what goes on in my novels. I've always found in my fiction that I like to explore very long periods of time, and to get a sense of the character's whole life, whole decades going by. And one or two of the poems, I think, have that feeling.

JA: There is one poem that stuck me in particular, which perhaps is slightly different from the model I was just describing. It is called "Borrowers" and it played on the word "credit," and the first of it is, I think, kind of prescient given the credit crunch that seems to be enveloping us. So I guess my stunning second question is, you've seen to have known about this all along and you didn't try to tell anyone? [laughter]

GS: Well, I don't think it was prescience. I mean that poem, like the other poems, would have been written in fact a few years ago, so before what is happening now in the financial world. But I think what is happening now is only the fruit, the bad fruit of what was going on then, which was indeed a great deal of borrowing, or over borrowing, and the use of credit; and in the poem, in fact, it has a rather retrospective element to it, even for the time in which it is written, or was written, and because it looks back to the time before the credit card. To a time before easy credit and to days in which the notion of living now and paying later was not current. It was the other way around if anything. And I'm old enough to remember such a time. I'm old enough to remember when there were no credit cards, and I've always felt they were—I have one myself of course—but I always felt they were rather dangerous things.

JA: I'd like to talk, to finish really, by talking about place, which, of course, comes up in your work, in your writings about your work, in your talking or describing your work a lot. I'm struck while reading the accounts of your friends, your writer friends in this book, people like Caryl Phillips, Rushdie, Ishiguru, Patrick McGrath. These are what we might call transnational writers. While you hail decisively, shall we say, from South London, and I believe you've lived mostly in that area.

GS: Still there. Yes, still there.

JA: Do you feel yourself then to be a London writer, an English writer, or a British writer, and if so what would that mean?

GS: I don't spend a lot of time feeling about, thinking about these kinds of labels. I'm a writer, basically, and I don't think I'm this kind of writer or that kind of writer. I'm obviously, if you want to call me this, an English writer, because I'm indisputably English, and I come from London. I was born in London. I've lived in London most of my life. And this is reflected to some considerable measure in my work. It's also, incidentally, one reason why I'm glad my archive is here in London. It's just kind of up the road for me. But I don't feel, I don't feel my sort of geographical confines actually to be particularly confined because, fortunately, I know that my work is read in many parts of the world, both in its original English form, in North America for example, and is read in translation in all kinds of countries. So, something about my work must travel, even though it may be at the same time quite English, it may have a quality that goes from where it comes from. But I hope I'm touching on some sort of universal themes, some things which are true for human beings wherever they are. And, in that sense, perhaps I do transcend my origins. I'm not a great traveler. I like traveling, and, in fact, one way or the other I have traveled, I suppose, a lot. But I think what I do do is actually travel a lot in my head. And the traveling that a writer does is not necessarily from one country to another. It's from one character to another. And the great excitement and adventure of writing is really getting out of yourself, your own circumstances, into someone else's. And that someone else might be on the other side of the world, they might be just around the corner. But it's still the same kind of adventure. It's still the same big journey.

JA: Talking about translation, transposition, I haven't seen, I still haven't seen the film of *Waterland*. But I was surprised, shocked to find out from the book, that the bits of the book that were set in the novel in Greenwich and London were transposed to, I think, Pennsylvania.
GS: To Pittsburgh.

JA: Yes, Pittsburgh to be precise. Yeah . . . How on earth did that come about? How did it affect the balance of the film? And how did your idea of time, of Greenwich meantime, affect knowing it was going to be set in Pittsburgh?
GS: Well, I would have to say I was shocked as well at the time. The circumstances were that, at times, this is the first adaptation of a book of mine. I was not at all well versed in these things. It was in the hands of the film production company. I went away, carried on with my writing. Half-thinking, more than half-thinking, that the film would never be made. And suddenly it was being made, and suddenly I was aware of all kinds of things, including the fact that a large part of the film was going to be set in America. And I literally became aware of this when I was invited to a day of shooting on location in Norfolk. I discovered this at a point where it was obviously an absolute *fait accompli*. There was nothing I could do about it. The cameras were already rolling, if they were rolling in England at that time. And I don't think it would have helped anyone, and, in a way, least of all me, if I sort of created an enormous tantrum about it. It was just a fact. It doesn't totally destroy the film. I think the best parts of the film are. . . are the parts that are set in England. And it's a very sincerely made film; it has real strengths. Looking back, I wish I had been more involved in the adaptation process, so that hopefully I could have controlled such things. Being a bit more, sort

of, crude and materialistic about it, it was, it had American money in it. It had an American director. They were thinking of the American market. So they thought, let's get an American angle on this film. And I dare say there were also some interesting tax breaks involved, shooting some scenes in Pittsburgh, so that's going to happen.

JA: Okay. One penultimate question, it kind of leads on from place. It's about where real life butts against fiction and vice versa. You mention that novel writing is about making imaginative leaps and connecting people through imagination, characters through imagination. Two stories I've seen recently, one was a debate that *The Guardian* editorialized about, over whether one should be allowed to throw ashes, human ashes, in public spaces as an act of memorial, and *Last Orders* was brought into the narrative. And secondly, I read a writer who was traveling around Norfolk and the Fens, and talked about Graham Swift's Fens, knowing you don't come from that area. How does it feel when unintentionally and unimaginably, your fictional creations surge up within real life narrative?

GS: I would have to say that it's one of the delights and thrills of a writing life that this sort of thing, again, which, when I set off as a writer, I never would have imagined. I am generally a writer who I would say is non-autobiographical. I do not use my own direct experiences to turn into my novels. But there are other ways in which fact and fiction collide. And it is the case that truth is sometimes stranger than fiction, and it's also the case that I know that I bump into my fiction, as you say, within the real context, and it brings me up with a jolt. But it's a rather delightful jolt. And the feeling that my work is somehow mixed with reality, is actually a very pleasing one.

JA: One final question then that looks toward the future. One of the great things with the archives of living writers is, of course, that the archives themselves are expanding, and so in a year or so, a year or two, we hope to be able to get the drafts of your next novel, which I believe you are working on. I just wondered, your novels have been getting more and more concise, I think. *Ever After* was a day I guess, *Last Orders* was a day, and *Tomorrow* was a night. Is the new novel continuing in that direction? Or is it back to the expansiveness of *Waterland*?

GS: I think there is a limit to that process. You have a novel which occupies the space of half an hour. The novel I'm now working on, and it's still in a fairly amorphous state, so I have to be careful what I say about it. But I don't see it as reducing the time span any further. Although I think the way it might shape up is that it will have, as well as a lot of other stuff which takes place in long periods of time, long periods of memory, certain events which occur in quite a narrow period of time. Anyway, in this case maybe the space of two or three days, which is actually rather longer than the night, the single night in *Tomorrow*. I seem to be drawn to that sort of duality, of a narrative which is both very immediate and occupying immediate periods of hours or days, and yet at the same time is historically quite big, quite long, quite backward looking.

JA: Do you have a title, a working title, while you're composing?
GS: In this case, no.

JA: Do you have . . .
GS: Sometimes the title has come to me quite quickly. I've thought why I'm now writing this thing which has a name. Currently I have no title. It doesn't bother me. It doesn't bother me if it isn't discovered until I've finished. It's, it's . . . I think with *The Light of Day* I had a sense of that would be its title, because I had a sense that those would be the last words of the novel. That was rather peculiar. *Waterland* was not a title I had until after I'd finished. *Last Orders* came to me at some point in the course of writing, quite late in the course of writing. But it came to me as the obvious title for the new book. I mean it just leapt out at me. Peculiar things titles.

JA: Well, whatever its title, we look forward to welcoming it to the archives. And Graham Swift, thank you very much.
GS: Thank you.

Kirkus Q&A with Graham Swift

Don McLeese / 2012

From *Kirkus Reviews* 80.9 (2012): 904. Reprinted by permission of the author.

The richness of everyday life provides seemingly inexhaustible possibility within the novels of Graham Swift, whose *Wish You Were Here* ranks with his best. It's a novel of rural England, where destinies appear to be preordained, yet every life, and every decision within it, so profoundly affects so many others.

A man mourns the death of his brother, a soldier in Iraq with whom he'd lost contact, and the delicate balance of his existence begins to topple, threatening everything from his marriage to his memories. Few novelists show more subtle mastery than Swift, whose characters invite the reader's empathy rather than judgment.

Q: What was the seed of inspiration for this novel?
A: I never have a grand plan. Novels for me arise obscurely and with a strong sense of the provisional. There eventually comes a point when I know I'm "in" one, but not how I've crossed the threshold. I may well have begun with the shotgun—the shotgun that features in the opening pages and has several appearances in the book, in the hands of different characters.

Q: How did the topical element of Iraq and the "war on terror" in this novel change the writing experience?
A: It all came from my groping for the story behind that first scene. I felt that as well as telling the story of a man and wife, the novel would involve the relationship of two brothers, that there'd be a missing brother—Tom— who'd be much younger than the main character, Jack. I can't explain why at some point I made the leap to the missing brother having joined the army many years ago, thus to Iraq and thus to what became the spine of the narrative—the almost literal "coming home" of that war, the story of

the return of a dead soldier. But I can't stress too much how all this, with its political, even global implications, arose out of a local, intimate context. This is a novel about farming as much as anything, about all the meanings the word "land" can have, including that of close, heartbreaking physical view. I seem to write novels that are simultaneously domestic and undomestic, rooted and uprooted.

Q: Why did Jack and his wife come together, and why have they stayed together"
A: They plainly weren't brought together in any greatly romantic way, more by geographical circumstance and by their limited range of choices, but this is only how many unions are made that prove long lasting. Their relationship has its strengths, its depths and its significant weaknesses . . . I love them both and their seldom-articulated, stubborn love for each other. All this said, it's clear from the beginning that their relationship has never been so severely tested as now.

Q: Were you conscious of wanting to write something with more of an element of suspense? Are the pacing and chronological structure organic to this novel?
A: I hope all my novels involve a degree of suspense, if only because storytelling, the process of gradual revelation, is inherently suspenseful. But it's true that the final chapters of *Wish You Were Here* have a strong "cliffhanger" element. Many readers have commented on the roller coaster experience, on how they absolutely couldn't guess the outcome. I can only say I shared all this myself. I really didn't know at the beginning how it would end.

Q: Do you think English readers and American ones might identify differently with your novels in general and this one in particular?
A: Because I try to write about core human stuff and because I believe in empathy, I'd hope the differences are minor. Novels have to be set somewhere, and I've said elsewhere, though it's hardly my original thought, that the local is the route to the universal.

"When You're Reading a Book, You're On a Little Island"

Susanna Rustin / 2014

From *The Guardian* July 5, 2014. Reprinted by permission of The Guardian.

Graham Swift's new collection of short stories—his first for more than thirty years—is called *England and Other Stories*, and "England" is the name of the last one in the book. In it a coastguard, Ken, driving across Exmoor at 5 a.m., stops to help the driver of a beaten-up BMW stuck in a gully at the side of the road. The stranger turns out to be an African-Caribbean comedian from West Yorkshire, stranded on his way to a booking in Ilfracombe on the north Devon coast, and the story turns on Ken's perception of him. Where is he from? Could he be dangerous? Is he lying when he says he swerved to avoid a deer? Is he even real? "In time even Johnny Dewhurst, like that questionable deer, might start to seem like a hallucination," Ken tells himself as he drives off into the dawn, having resolved to tell nobody about the encounter and to decline an invitation to that night's show for fear of becoming part of the routine ("Have you heard the one about the lost coastguard?").

"It's a totally bizarre story, I went with its bizarreness," says Swift. "I suppose of all the stories in the book it is the most weirdly many-faceted. It brings together so many diverse things in, of all places, Exmoor."

Swift, who is sixty-five, grew up in south Croydon, Greater London, and has lived in the same house in the capital for decades with his wife, whom he met when both were students in York, but whose childhood home was in the adjoining suburb, Thornton Heath. Swift, who came from a modest background and attended the private school Dulwich College on a scholarship, is a south Londoner to his bones. He loves it, and says: "Out of all the big metropolitan cities in the world, London has probably absorbed diversity within itself the best."

But he recognizes the capital's apartness from the rest of the UK. One of his two most successful novels, 1983's *Waterland,* was set in the Fens. The other, 1996's Booker prize-winning *Last Orders,* he has called a "tribute" to Kent. While the mood of his writing about London is often celebratory –the first story in the new book, "Going Up in the World," is about a window cleaner who has made a fortune washing skyscrapers—in other settings feelings of unease and alienation come to the fore.

"All these stories are bits of England but they are bits of different Englands," he says. "England now is such a heterogenous, indefinable place. I like the title *England and Other Stories* because what a lot of people think of as England may be just a story now. I myself am obviously unequivocally and indigenously English, I was born in England and I'm very attached to my country. But I think as a writer all the time I'm approaching it as though it might be a strange place."

He dates his own urge to write to his contented childhood. The younger of two sons of a Royal Navy fighter pilot, who in peacetime became a civil service clerk, and a stay-at-home-mother, he is a baby boomer with a powerful sense of his own good luck. He went to university in Cambridge and York, travelled on his own for a while in Greece, and had no trouble picking up the casual teaching work that saw him through his twenties.

"I often write about the moments of crisis in people's live where a space opens up," he says, "and it's strange because I think I identify with that quite strongly. But I am a very fortunate individual, I'm lucky I discovered what I wanted to do with my life and I am doing it, so I'm fulfilled and there aren't many people who can say that."

Swift's publishing career spans almost thirty-five years. His first novel, *The Sweet-Shop Owner,* was published in 1980 when he was thirty-one. By then he had destroyed several earlier efforts and acquired Alan Ross—the poet, *Observer* cricket correspondent and *London* magazine editor—as a patron. In his book of essays *Making an Elephant,* Swift described the impression made on him by this glamorous character who drank cocktails of gin and Campari, had a paperweight shaped like a woman's breast, and nude photographs on the walls of his south Kensington office.

But while magnetized by this glimpse of the world of books—and still keen on lunches, though publishing has moved on from the days of long, boozy meetings in restaurants—his fiction remained closely focused on the ordinary lives of undistinguished people. Or rather, people whose distinction was unnoticed by the world at large, but which it became Swift's mission to portray in his books.

We meet, at his suggestion, at St. Mary's Church, Putney, where he tells me that in the 1647 Putney debates, the radical Thomas Rainsborough argued that the poorest man in England had the same life to live as the greatest. Is Swift a republican, then? "In spirit," he says. "What does that mean in practical terms?"

But as we talk, first on a bench in Wandsworth park to the accompaniment of traffic noises and birdsong, and later over a meal, he explains that he isn't "the kind of writer who looks for issues" in the outside world; he sees instead "the stuff inside us." Nevertheless, literature does have a vital role beyond that. "We are bombarded by stories all the time, about what life is like and how we should live, whether they come from politicians or advertisers," he says. "I think we all know, unless we're stupid, that these stories are tosh. They are lies. What fiction can do is oppose all that and say: 'No, it's not like that, this is honestly what life is like, read my story,' you know? Without getting pompous about it, fiction can perform a very important moral and social function. It is highly democratic. You asked me if I'm a republican. I'm a republican certainly as a writer."

Swift belongs to the generation who revitalized British fiction during the 1980s and 1990s. In 1983, the year his magic-realist-inspired *Waterland* was shortlisted for the Booker—the winner that year was J. M. Coetzee—he was part of the now legendary lineup of "Young British Novelists" selected by *Granta* magazine that included Kazuo Ishiguro, Rose Tremain, Ian McEwan, Martin Amis, Pat Barker, Julian Barnes and Salman Rushdie.

Progress has not always been smooth. His most celebrated contributions remain *Waterland*, a murky tangle of familial rivalry, local history, eels and beer, and *Last Orders*, written soon after his father died of cancer, aged seventy, and Swift's elegy for a generation "who never got the breaks but lived with a surprising amount of humor and stoicism." A fine film version starred Helen Mirren, Bob Hoskins, David Hemmings, Bill Nighy [*sic*] and Michael Caine; when Caine accepted the role he said he had always known that he would end up playing his father, a Billingsgate porter.

Last Orders also occasioned a low point in Swift's working life when he was accused of having copied William Faulkner's *As I Lay Dying*. Swift now says the whole thing was "nonsense" cooked up by newspapers, but he does not deny Faulkner's influence and visited his grave in Mississippi on a book tour in the US.

Later novels have had mixed reviews, with some critics troubled by a perceived mismatch between what Tim Parks called Swift's "relentlessly literary" style and his characters. The stories in this latest book have most impact when they break new ground, as "England" does. Another story, "First on the Scene," would make a strong opening to a thriller. Swift says the experience of writing stories again has been "joyful," and cites recent awards, a Nobel prize for Alice Munro and the Folio prize for George Saunders, as signs of the form's resurgence. But he resists any suggestion of a conscious change of direction. While he talks with pride of how he made himself a writer through sheer determination, he regards fiction itself as beyond rational explanation. "I begin with nothing, or next to nothing. Some kind of flicker or tingle," he says. "People don't always like this word but it's done by art. There's some kind of ability on top of sheer instinct. You have to gradually understand it but it's art, and art is something some people have and some people don't. There's a word that's not used in this context anymore but it was used in the middle ages: mystery, to mean that craft, that thing. I like the double meaning of the word mystery, because it is both this thing that only some people have, but it is also a bloody mystery. I mean you can't analyze it, there's no formula."

Swift was influenced by Isaac Babel when he was younger, and kept a photograph of the Russian writer on his desk. Although "deeply attached" to the English language he sees himself as European and is against the decision to open the Man Booker prize to US writers. "Each prize has its own remit, why expand it?" he asks. "It's like saying at the Commonwealth Games, 'Let's have the Americans!' The reverse is not the case: the Pulitzer prize is not open to British writers. It's almost like saying they deserve to win the prize, and I don't think so." Swift writes about the fissures and catastrophes between people: the betrayals, disappointments and fallings-out of relationships. But he believes that fiction can heal these rifts and misunderstandings, or at least make them less painful. "I love them all, even the ones who are not so likable," he says of his characters. "I think that's a condition of writing. You must basically love the people. That doesn't mean a soppy kind of love, it means a respecting kind of love that acknowledges who they are."

"When you're reading a book, you're on a little island, but this thing that is made and received in isolation is working against isolation," he says. "It really is working towards real human communion, not of a silly public kind but real. You can't see what goes on when someone reads a book but it's all about sharing, fundamentally, saying to your reader, 'Look, I'm in the same boat, that's the spirit!'"

Graham Swift's New Novel Shows Exactly How One Event Can Shape a Whole Life

Max Liu / 2016

From *The Independent* (Feb. 16, 2016) © Independent 2018. Reprinted by permission of *ESI Media: The Independent and London Evening Standard.*

Interviews can be nerve-racking affairs, but, as I wait for Graham Swift at a crowded Soho restaurant, I feel especially apprehensive. Reading interviews with him, I sense that, although polite and thoughtful, Swift finds discussing his work a chore. Not only that—Jane, the protagonist of his new novel, *Mothering Sunday*, regards "interview chicanery" and "bothersome questions" as the banes of a writer's life. Still, I hear Swift enjoys the kind of long lunch that's synonymous with literary London's past and, when he arrives, dressed in a black suit and white shirt, he asks with some relish: "So, we're going to eat and drink, then?"

He suggests we start with champagne and, once we've clinked flutes, I ask if he was trying, in his new novel, to make himself interview-proof. "No," he says, "there's no agenda and Jane isn't me. But many things in life cannot be explained. The stories in my previous book, *England and Other Stories* (2014), came to me inexplicably. I hadn't written stories for decades and then suddenly I was writing lots. With *Mothering Sunday*, there was no premeditation. One day I had nothing and the next day I was working on it. I can describe this process but I can't explain it."

Swift, who speaks softly, goes to his desk every morning at five-thirty: "I feel I should be at my post to see if anything happens." Born in 1949, in London, as a child he found reading magical: "I wanted to be part of the magic so becoming a writer was my dream," he says. "But I was aware of my dream's fragility. Nobody in my family was interested in writing and

149

I didn't know if I had any talent." His first novel, *The Sweet-Shop Owner*, appeared in 1980 and his third, *Waterland* (1983), established him among a golden generation of British novelists which also included his friends Kazuo Ishiguro and Salman Rushdie. Today, Swift lives with his wife ("my first and most stringent reader") in southwest London. "I thrive on the city," he says. "It still surprises me."

His enthusiasm for writing is undimmed too. "For the year I spent working on *Mothering Sunday*," he says, "I felt I was writing it in one breath and I was writing it to be read in one breath." It's his tenth and shortest novel, so does brevity inevitably appeal to older writers? "The reason why you write something short is that there's no reason to write something longer. There are things you write later in life that you could not have written earlier. *Mothering Sunday* is a physically small book but its embrace is very big."

Jane's story is told in close third-person narration which feels so intimate that some readers have, Swift says, mistaken it for first person. It's masterfully structured, with Jane reflecting from her nineties on a pivotal day in her early-twenties. Time collapses across a century to show how a single event can have ramifications for a whole life. "I began with the young lovers, Jane and Paul, in bed," Swift says when I ask how he started their story. "I knew there was some social difference between them which meant their affair was secret. Questions came from my unconscious: Where and when is this happening? Somewhere in the Home Counties on a gorgeously warm day in 1924. I decided Jane was a maid and Paul was a young master who was engaged to another woman. They were meeting across the divide. It had to be Mothering Sunday when everyone else was out."

On Mothering Sunday, Jane's fellow servants are "out in the world . . . being reminded that they had lives, even mothers, of their own." As an orphan, Jane is the exception with nowhere to go. She seeks solace in books, which she borrows from her employer's library, and will eventually become a writer, so is Swift saluting the autodidact tradition? "No, no, no," he says, appalled by the suggestion that Jane could be anything other than exceptional. "Jane's reading is simply down to her native gumption."

Nobody, however, exists in a vacuum and *Mothering Sunday*, like Swift's Booker Prize-winning novel *Last Orders* (1996), takes place at a moment of social upheaval. "I have, without planning it," he says, "set novels on the cusp of historical changes. The first half of the 1920s is interesting because there's grief about the First World War mixed with the emergence of the modern world. *Last Orders* was about a generation who'd been shaped by the Second World War, growing old in the early-1980s. The world of that book has receded but any point in history can become a moment of change in hindsight."

Mothering Sunday is, Swift says, "quite a sexy novel" but his characters' nakedness is symbolic too. Jane and Paul lie together in "the perfect politics of nakedness" and Swift says: "When Paul has to go out to meet his fiancée, he leaves Jane on her own. She wanders about and sees the house without its usual hierarchies. At the same time, she's looking at her own true, naked self, without the social definitions which imprison her. When she puts her clothes on, she leaves the house in this wonderful atmosphere of possibility. It's a kind of rebirth and, although she doesn't know it yet, she will make something of her life."

Swift is good company and, with the plates cleared (we both had the tuna steak) and the wine nearly all gone, conversation is relaxed. He tells me he chose Modigliani's "Reclining Nude" for his novel's cover because "it's perfect," that he's reading the Dutch novelist Gerbrand Bakker and that seeing his own work translated is one of the joys of being a writer: "I feel like I belong to other languages." Would he vote to stay in the European Union? "My heart is always for being part of Europe. England, or Britain, is in its roots much more integrated with Europe than many people admit. The English language is a wonderful amalgam of other languages and is in itself a continent."

More than once, Swift expresses his love for fiction: "It is a great thing and, if it works, it has immediacy whenever or wherever it's set." He believes writing is about "harnessing that inexplicable something behind words which gives simple sentences enormous power." Does he love his characters? "Everything I've written is close to me. If the characters from *Last Orders* walked in now, I wouldn't be surprised. I never imagined that the people in my books would still be there for me long after I'd finished writing about them. But they are."

Graham Swift and the Power of the Imagination

Jason Steger / 2016

From *The Sydney Morning Herald* (March 7, 2016). https://www.smh.com.au/entertainment /books/graham-swift-and-the-power-of-the-imagination-20160307-gnccqx.html. Reprinted by permission of *The Sydney Morning Herald*. The use of this work has been licensed by Copyright Agency except as permitted by the Copyright Act, you must not reuse this work without the permission of the copyright owner or Copyright Agency.

When Graham Swift answers the phone in his south London home early on a February morning, it's only just light outside and the night's chill is preserving the sheen of frost on the grass.

We are going to talk about his latest novel, more a novella really, *Mothering Sunday: A Romance*. It is the story of Jane Fairchild, an orphan who works as a housemaid in a country house in England's Home Counties in 1924. She has no mother to visit this last Sunday of March, a day when servants are traditionally allowed a half day free, and so spends the time in the bed of her lover, Paul Sheringham, the only surviving son and now sole heir to a nearby estate.

After a seven-year, secret affair, it is their last time together as he is shortly to be married. But for now they have—thrillingly and for the first time—the house entirely to themselves. She can lie in his bed and let her eyes linger on him as he dresses to go to meet his fiancée at a nearby hotel. And, once he has left, she can wander naked—daring and brazen—through the stately rooms downstairs before taking her leave of the house forever.

It is a day that will come to change both their lives, a day that she will never forget. It is a day with a story that she will never tell, even when in later life she has become a famous novelist.

Graham Swift says the main characters in his novels remain close to him.

At one point Swift pictures her being celebrated in her old age, at seventy-five, at eighty, "batting away the same old questions" from journalists. So I wondered whether it was right to be nervous about talking to him, whether he had that same dislike of the round of interviews on publication of a book. "I wouldn't worry about that; Jane's not me."

Mothering Sunday is a deceptive book, short, carefully structured and full. The reader is allowed to see Jane's past and glimpse into her future.

"She is a woman who lives to be almost a hundred so in theory I could have taken her at a point late in her life and had her looking back over her life and indeed her long career as a writer. But I absolutely never wanted to do that," Swift says.

Jane is already a reader, borrowing books from her employer's library at Beechwood. She has an appreciation of language and story. Words are like an invisible skin, she says at one point, giving the world reality.

"She's certainly the vessel of her own imagination. That is to say she is clearly aware or sensitive to things, experiences and a lot's going to happen on this day which does indeed fuel and feed the business of fiction and storytelling," her creator says.

Swift is the author of ten novels, a book of essays and three collections of short stories. He is probably best known for his third novel, *Waterland*, and *Last Orders*, for which he won the Booker Prize in 1996.

In the introduction to the twenty-fifth anniversary edition of *Waterland*, which was first published in 1983, he writes of a "guiding instinct" to his fiction: "One begins with the ordinary, mundane, even disappointing world we all know and looks for the extraordinary in it."

Instinct and imagination are words he uses most when discussing his writing. How he narrates his books are "very instinctive decisions" and "I used to have instincts about writing and then sort of question them. I realize now that there's no point in questioning them because the important thing is to trust them."

He regularly disappoints people who talk to him about *Waterland* when he tells them he has no personal connection with the Fens, the low-lying part of eastern England where this novel of history, beer and, improbably, eels, was set. It was down to his imagination.

"The imagination can do remarkable things. I believe that it can even take you to the truth about things, about things of which even you don't have direct personal experience yourself."

Sometimes it can even surprise him. Take *Mothering Sunday*. "I wasn't sitting around thinking 'oh, I'd like to write a story about a housemaid' or anything like that.' One day it wasn't there, the next day it was. That is actually quite often how it is. If such things couldn't occur so unexpectedly and inexplicably then writing would be far less exciting than it can be.

"It's very hard to convince people—they tend not to believe you. I start with nothing and I make something. That's the whole joy and challenge and often frustration of it. I don't start with something that is as it were already there and I then process it. I start from nothing."

History—personal, emotional and literal—has always been an important element in his fiction. E. H. Carr, the British historian of Soviet Russia, once said it was a dialogue between the past and the present but in *Mothering Sunday* the dialogue is between the past, present and the future.

"I think it's a novel about becoming . . . to put it crudely and simply, it's about a housemaid who becomes an eminent writer. This is why I give the thing the epigraph, the line everyone knows from *Cinderella*. ['You shall go to the ball.']

"That's a joyous expression of things being fulfilled, of things coming about. And I think that is a strong emotional force in the novel; it's about potential, possibility. It's about how some individuals can emerge from themselves and while they remain themselves they do become a sort of new enhanced creature. And it's a wonderful thing."

You get the impression that Swift is wedded to the value of fiction. He didn't come from a family of writers; he was inspired by reading children's books and the magic stuff he found inside. To be a writer was a dream he clung to while he resisted his "rather boring conventional background that would have sent me in another direction."

He started to write stories in his late teens but kept them to himself. It was a long apprenticeship, he says, before he felt any of it was good enough to get published.

"It was a long slow haul. This only stresses that it was all down to me; it all came from me. No one was pushing me in this direction except myself."

His first novel to be published was *The Sweet-Shop Owner* in 1980. *Waterland*, which many considered worthy of the Booker, his third in 1983. But it was a good time to be writing, he reckons, because that decade saw a general renaissance of the novel in Britain: "There was a feeling in the air about fiction and the novel which was quite exciting."

It was in 1983 that *Granta* produced its first list of best young British novelists. Swift featured, as did Ian McEwan, Julian Barnes, Rose Tremain, Salman Rushdie and Kazuo Ishiguro. "A lot of us still seem to be going fairly strong," he notes.

The timing was right when he won the Booker because by the time of *Last Orders* he had a fair amount of experience under his belt and could enjoy it. "If I had won it [for *Waterland*] it might have unbalanced me a bit in my career."

He still sees writing as an insecure and difficult profession but suggests young writers face additional problems these days. "I think the big change occurred in the publishing world. Publishers once were genuinely interested in fostering a writer for a whole career if they felt they had it in them . . . the publisher may not be interested anymore even though the writer might have a great deal of genuine potential."

Swift talks with great affection for his books and has the feeling everything he writes is in a kind of present tense: "So the main characters in novels I would have written now decades ago are still as present for me as much more recent ones."

McEwan once said that when he finished a novel, the characters were dead to him, an idea that is anathema to Swift.

"The main characters [of my novels] are very close to me still. I know this sounds slightly mad, but I have a feeling that some of them exist outside the novels in which they made their actual appearance. It wouldn't be totally crazy if one day I met them."

It is a lovely thought to imagine Swift encountering Jane Fairchild as either a housemaid with a long life ahead of her or as a venerable novelist. But then he adds: "I know this can't occur."

Index

Sterne, Laurence, 6, 41; *Tristram Shandy*, 90
Stone, Robert, 74
Swift, Graham: on abortion, 23; on advice to writers, xiii, 53–54, 59, 83, 89, 155; on archive, 131–32, 135–37; on authority of writer, 44; on autobiographical elements in fiction, ix, xiii, 16, 31, 47, 59, 64–65, 83–84, 89–90, 105, 108, 122, 141, 148, 153; on Booker Prize, x–xi, 18, 55, 58–59, 68, 100, 147, 155; on books, 75, 154; on borders, 64; on boys' adventure stories, 57, 154; on British writers, 7, 18–19, 139; on characters, xiii, 4, 22, 30, 33, 36, 47–49, 50, 53, 55, 56, 59, 60, 62, 65, 72–73, 76, 84–85, 88, 90, 91, 96, 98, 108–9, 111, 147–48, 150, 151–52, 155; on childhood, xi, 4, 8, 11, 17, 31, 50, 56, 64–65, 83–84, 87, 97, 123–24, 139, 146, 154; on Cold War, 100; on compassion, 40, 93, 108; on complexity, 64; on contemporary fiction, xiii–xiv, 6–7, 28, 39, 42, 44, 51–52, 59, 61, 75, 84, 104, 154; on critics and reviewers, 51, 61, 79–80, 95, 97; on death, xiv, 4, 14, 31, 33, 35, 49, 55–56, 66, 85, 88; on detective fiction, 24, 76–77; on the divine, 38–39; on early career, ix, xi, 4–5, 17, 29, 50, 56–57, 83–84, 121–22, 125–26, 145–49, 154; on education, xi, 11, 39, 50–52, 57, 121, 145–46; on emotion, 16, 38, 41, 63, 81; on empathy, 40, 45, 53, 59, 64, 93, 108, 140, 144, 148; on empire, 102; on English language, 151; on the environment, 101; on escapism, 53; on evolution of work, 106; on fairy tales, 23; on farming, 144; on financial crisis, 138–39; on finishing a novel, 78–79, 105, 133, 144; on fishing, xii, 24, 35, 128–30, 135; on function of literature, 61; on generational conflict, 88, 150–51; on history, 14, 21–22, 24, 27, 31, 34–35, 40, 52, 61–62, 65–66, 86–88, 100–101, 104, 138, 142, 150–51, 154; on humor, 8, 41, 49, 56, 66, 96; on hybridity, 64; on identity, xi, 28, 31–32, 38–39, 45, 63, 139, 146; on ideology, 102; on individualism of writing, 61; on inspiration for novels, xi, 14, 24, 30, 47, 56, 66, 78, 81, 85, 101, 135, 143–44, 148–50, 153–54; on instinct, xiii, 8, 32, 41, 53, 56, 65, 78, 110, 126, 133, 148, 153; on interviewing, ix–xi, 3, 9, 96, 120, 149, 153; on invisibility of writer, ix, 61, 69–70; on irony, 64; on journalism, 84, 104, 135, 153; on knowing, 22, 25; on libraries, 75; on literary agents, 70; on literary culture, 76; on literary friendships, 29, 79, 105, 131, 135–36, 139; on literary influences, x–xi, 5–6, 41–42, 48–49, 59, 84–85, 147; on literary tradition, 39–42, 63, 147; on loss, 66; on love, 32, 66, 68, 73, 96–97, 107, 144, 148, 151, 152; on madness and mental hospitals, 9, 15–16, 17, 35, 57; on magic and magical realism, 26, 28, 45, 56, 59, 61, 86–87, 89, 147, 149, 154; on manuscripts, 132–34, 137; on marriage, xii, 25, 73; on meaning of life, 52–53;

on memory, 22; on mixing of genres, 60; on modernism, 84, 87; on morality, 40; on mortality, 33; on murder mysteries, 77; on music, 36, 43, 62, 81; on mystery, 148; on narrators, 4, 21–22, 30–31, 35–37, 56, 60, 62, 71–72, 90–92, 97–98, 106, 150; on nature, 22–23; on novel as film, xii, 75, 77, 92, 98, 120, 140–41; on novel genre, 4, 8; on the ordinary, xii, 16, 30, 47, 71–72, 78, 84, 146, 153; on originality, 63; on parent relationships, 17, 31, 39, 64, 72–73, 83, 85, 97, 123–24, 127, 132, 146–47; on parts of novel, xiv, 3–4, 8, 17, 21–23, 24–27, 30, 32, 35, 36–38, 39, 42–44, 45, 48, 49, 52, 55–56, 60, 62–63, 64, 65–66, 67, 68, 72–73, 76, 78, 86, 88, 90, 95, 97–98, 100, 102, 105, 107, 108, 138, 140, 141–42, 143–44, 146, 148–51, 153, 154; on place, 39, 89–90, 99, 106, 139, 146; on plagiarism, x; on poetry, xii, 13–14, 32, 61, 127, 129, 137–39; on politics, xiii, 102–3, 144, 147, 151; on publishing, ix–x, 3, 18, 68–71, 75, 80, 155; on readers, 49–51, 58, 61–63, 65–66, 69–70, 74–76, 79–80, 92–93, 96–97, 105, 108, 139, 144, 148, 150, 153; on realism, 23, 28, 30–32, 35, 64, 124, 141, 153; on religion, 39; on sentiment, 33; on short stories, 148; on silence, 22–23, 26, 30, 63; on spies, 31; on storytelling, xiii, 3–4, 14, 21, 23, 27, 30, 35, 45–46, 52–53, 61–62, 66, 81, 87–88, 91, 138, 143–44, 152–53; on style, xi–xii, 12–13, 32, 35, 38–39, 44, 57, 59–60, 63, 67, 72, 74, 84,

91–92, 106, 132–33, 147, 151, 153; on supernatural, 23, 26; on superstition, 23, 27; on suspense, 144; on teaching, xii, 11–12, 52, 57, 73, 88–89, 96; on translation of works, 3, 28, 80, 139–40, 151; on travel, xi–xii, 59, 80–81, 85, 121, 139–40, 146; on twentieth century, 87; on universality of experience, 66, 85–86, 140, 144; on water, 55, 100–101, 130, 138; on writing as act of imagination, xi–xiii, 16, 26, 31, 40, 53–54, 56, 58–59, 64–65, 83, 89–90, 122, 124, 141, 151, 153–54; on writing process, xii, xiii, 7, 29, 32, 57–58, 68–69, 78–79, 86, 122–23, 126, 132, 133–35, 138, 148

Nonfiction
Making an Elephant, xii–xiii, 99, 120, 122, 127–28, 130, 132, 137–38, 146; "The Bookmark," 127; "Borrowers," 138

Novels
Ever After, 9, 30–33, 35, 37–39, 60, 66–67, 95, 106–7, 136, 141
Last Orders, x, xiii–xiv, 34–35, 47–49, 55, 60, 66–68, 72, 78, 82–83, 85–86, 90–91, 94–95, 98, 100, 106, 120, 141–42, 146–47, 150–51, 153
Light of Day, The, 9, 67–68, 72, 76, 78, 80, 94–95, 104, 106–7, 137, 142
Mothering Sunday, ix, xiii–xiv, 149–54
Out of this World, 31, 34–35, 63, 67, 83, 102
Shuttlecock, xi, 3, 5, 15–16, 31, 33–34, 38, 55, 60, 63, 67, 90, 95
Sweet-Shop Owner, The, 3, 5, 34, 62, 67, 95, 106–7, 146, 150, 154

About the Editor

Image credit: Louisiana Tech University,
Donny J. Crowe

Donald P. Kaczvinsky is the George E. Pankey Eminent Scholar in English and Dean of the College of Liberal Arts at Louisiana Tech University. He has published extensively on twentieth-century British literature, with a specialization in the Modern and Contemporary novel. His scholarly writing includes books and articles on such writers as James Joyce, Lawrence Durrell, Alasdair Gray, and Graham Swift.